ARE THESE THE LAST DAYS?

Robert Glenn Gromacki

Regular Baptist Press
1300 North Meacham Road
Post Office Box 95500
Schaumburg, Illinois 60195

To
my children,
Gary and Gail

All Scripture quotations in this volume are from the *King James Version of the Bible.*

Acknowledgment for the use of "He Is Coming Again" by Mabel Camp is extended to Singspiration, Inc. Copyright 1913. Renewal 1941 by Norman H. Camp. Assigned to Singspiration, Inc. All rights reserved. Used by permission.

Acknowledgment for the use of "What If It Were Today" by Leila N. Morris is extended to Hope Publishing Co. Copyright by Hope Publishing Co. Used by permission.

Library of Congress Cataloging in Publication Data

Gromacki, Robert Glenn.
    Are these the last days?

    1. Bible—Prophecies. 2. Second Advent. I. Title.
BS647.2.G76 1978   236   75-42165
ISBN 0-87227-019-X

©1970
Regular Baptist Press
Schaumburg, Illinois
Printed in the U.S.A.
All rights reserved.
Third printing—1978

CONTENTS

1 – WHY STUDY PROPHECY?

EVERYONE IS interested in the future. The little boy wonders what he will be when he grows up—explorer, astronaut or pro football player. The teenager dreams about her Prince Charming—"What will he be like? How many children will I have?" The athlete is concerned whether he will make the football or basketball team. Parents hope that their children will be successful and not disappointments, falling short of their expectations.

The nation listens to the economists who predict about the future of the dollar, inflation, depression, and the rise and fall of stocks. The sociologist warns about continued racial strife unless pockets of ghetto poverty are removed through urban renewal, housing integration, and improved educational facilities. The historian echoes the past as he points to the future—the rise and fall of nations plus the goal of history. What about tomorrow's weather? Everyone is interested in that! Will it be sunny? Rain? Snow? That is why all newscasts contain weather outlooks. Pity the poor weatherman if they don't come to pass.

In all of these predictions and future hopes, there are doubts and disagreements. The future is too misty and shadowy to be dogmatic about it. Yet there is a definite word about the future, as sure as the present and as foundational as the past. It is found in God's Word, the Bible. Only God is omniscient. He knows everything—the past, the present and the future. Moreover, He has chosen to reveal much of the future to us through the inscribed Word of God. Moses said, "The secret things belong unto the LORD our God: but those things which are revealed belong unto us and to our children for ever" (Deut. 29:29). Paul added:

> But as it is written, Eye hath not seen, nor ear heard, neither have entered into the heart of man, the things which God hath prepared for them that love him.

> But God hath revealed them unto us by his Spirit: for the Spirit searcheth all things, yea, the deep things of God (1 Cor. 2:9, 10).

Man, in himself, is not able to control or to discern the future. Nor is he able to understand fully the Bible by himself. The Scripture, including the prophetic utterances, did not originate within the thought processes or desires of men, but rather "holy men of God spake as they were moved by the Holy Ghost" (2 Pet. 1:21). Therefore, the Bible cannot be privately interpreted (2 Pet. 1:20). In order to know the Biblical message, one must be holy even as the Biblical authors were. The interpreter must be directed by the indwelling Holy Spirit of God just as the Biblical prophets. It is possible to know the future, but only as one is properly related to the Holy Spirit who will exclusively communicate spiritual truth to hearts that are spiritually prepared (1 Cor. 2:14, 15). Jesus Christ said that the Spirit would show believers "things to come" (John 16:13). Paul wrote that those who had received the Lord Jesus Christ as personal Savior from sin had "received, not the spirit of the world, but the spirit which is of God; that we might know the things that are freely given to us of God" (1 Cor. 2:12).

God, then, has done His part. He has revealed the program of the ages to the world through His written Word. Through the ministry of the Holy Spirit in the world and in the lives of Christians, man is able to know the future. Why then doesn't he? Why is he so ignorant of what God has said? In fact, why has his ignorance led to an open opposition to the study of prophecy?

Sad to say, some opposition has come from mistaken, although sincere, Christians. They admit that the Lord Jesus will one day come again to the earth, but in their immaturity, they claim that this is the only future event that can be known with certainty. Therefore, why study prophecy? It is full of symbols, metaphors and hard language. Instead of wrestling with the passage, they throw up their hands in utter despair.

Other Christians recognize the importance of Biblical prophecy, but in their zeal for noble goals, have relegated it to a low position on their scale of priorities. To them soul winning is the all-important passion of life. Visitation, tract distribution, soul-winning conferences and evangelistic meetings possess their lives. They simply have no time left for Bible study, especially that of prophecy. In a sense, they *may* look with suspicion upon the Christian who loves prophecy. They *may* regard him as a person who is failing the Great Commission and is not putting first things first. To others, the organization (local church, denomination, etc.) comes first. Emphasis upon the betterment of the present ministry of the church in the world has detracted from any interest in God's dramatic activity in the future.

Still other Christians look upon the study of Biblical prophecy as an academic area, reserved for the seminary classroom and for the course in eschatology (doctrine of last things). To them, it is just not practical, down-to-earth. They see no personal application to everyday living in such a study. In talking with many Christians, it is amazing to discover that few have attended prophetic conferences. Evangelistic and missionary conferences have been conducted in their home churches, but seldom a Bible or prophetic conference. Emphasis has been placed upon winning the lost and the nurturing of missionary zeal; edification of the saints through a practical knowledge of God's Word, including prophetic subjects, is minor.

Liberal theology naturally denies the value of studying Biblical prophecy. To them, the Bible is not God's Word, inscribed and inerrant; rather, it is a mere human book, complete with error and myth. Revelation of the future to man by a living God would be miraculous to them. Since they deny essential miracles, such as ex nihilo creation, the virgin birth and incarnation of Jesus Christ, His ministry of miracles, His substitutionary atonement for sin, His physical resurrection out of the dead and bodily ascension into Heaven, they naturally deny the fact of His physical return to the earth. To be consistent, study of future things as recorded in the Bible is practically valueless to them. Since they claim to be Biblical scholars, how do they explain the many prophetic passages? They state that the language is vague and/or that the prophecies were artificially fulfilled. By this they mean that the New Testament authors falsely applied the events of their day to be fulfillments of Old Testament prophecy. Many prophetic passages were written after the events had actually occurred. They late-date many books and passages (e.g., Isaiah 40—66; Daniel; prediction of the destruction of Jerusalem, Matthew 24, 25). To these scholars, the Biblical authors were men of their times writing prophecy because other prophets of other religions were doing the same thing. Within the scope of this chapter, it is impossible to answer these attacks upon the integrity of the Biblical record. Many excellent evangelical books have been written, disproving the attacks of these higher critics. Since these liberals have an anti-supernaturalistic bias, opposition from them must be expected. What Jesus said about the unbelieving religious scholars of His day can certainly be applied to those of this generation:

> . . . When it is evening, ye say, It will be fair weather: for the sky is red.
> And in the morning, It will be foul weather to day: for the sky is red and lowring. O ye hypocrites, ye can discern the face of the sky; but can ye not discern the signs of the times? (Matt. 16:2, 3).

There is also great indifference to Biblical prophecy on the part of the general populace. In their secularism and materialism, they are not too concerned about spiritual matters. They *are* concerned about the future, to the extent of pension, social security, and life insurance, but few have thought about "eternal life" insurance. To them, a prophet is a man, robed with black cloth, bearded, wearing sandals, walking down Main Street with a picket sign inscribed, "The end of the world is near." Biblical prophecy is likened to ESP, clairvoyance (a la Jeane Dixon) or crystal ball gazing. They are curious about it, but there is no serious interest; otherwise their Bibles would be opened rather than their daily horoscopes.

For the interested Christian, is there any legitimate basis for the study of Biblical prophecy? Are there any scriptural or practical reasons for such a study? What does the Bible have to say about it? First of all, Christians are exhorted to be students of the Word of God. Paul commanded: "Study to shew thyself approved unto God, a workman that needeth not to be ashamed, rightly dividing the word of truth" (2 Tim. 2:15). Peter admonished all to "desire the sincere milk of the word," in order to grow into spiritual maturity (1 Pet. 2:2). Since prophecy is part of God's Word, then the Christian is obligated to study it as well as the Ten Commandments or the Sermon on the Mount. At the time of writing, more than one-fourth (25 percent) of the Biblical text was prophetic in character, and much of that even today has been unfulfilled. If God has put so much prophecy in His Word, it stands to reason that the Christian should study it with as much vitality and desire as other sections.

Personal blessing can be gained through this type of study. The only book in the sacred canon that contains within it a blessing for the person who reads it is the Book of Revelation, and that certainly is a prophetic book! The apostle John, on the island of Patmos, began the Apocalypse with these words: "Blessed is he that readeth, and they that hear the words of this prophecy, and keep those things which are written therein: for the time is at hand" (Rev. 1:3). John, no doubt, was referring to the custom of the first-century churches where there was the reading of Scripture in the public worship service. Not everyone could read in those days so there were assigned readers in each congregation. Today many Christians own several versions of the English Bible, but in that time, there may have been only one copy (and that incomplete) per congregation. This is why a blessing was pronounced upon the *single* reader and the *plural* hearers of the book. Since most people have Bibles today and can read, certainly the blessing extends to all believers. Also, how could a blessing belong to those who would *keep* the contents of the book if they could not understand what to keep? John ended his book with similar words (Rev. 22:7), adding a warning given to him: "Seal not the sayings of the prophecy of this book: for the time is at hand" (Rev. 22:10). Revelation, like all other prophetic books, is an *open* book, open to study, to understanding and to blessing. It was not always so.

When Daniel finished writing his strongly prophetic book, he was confused and curious about its contents. When he inquired about them, he was told: "Go thy way, Daniel: for the words are closed up and sealed till the time of the end" (Dan. 12:8, 9). What Daniel and other prophets could not understand about Biblical prophecy because of time perspective and partial revelation (1 Pet. 1:10-12), we Christians *now* can understand. We have a complete revelation (all sixty-six books); much has been fulfilled. We have the advantage of time; we can see the divine rationale behind the fulfilled prophecies, and we can gain personal blessing by reading of God's future goals.

Prophecy does have practical value. Knowledge of the future can give present comfort and hope to the child of God. The night before His crucifixion, Jesus told His disciples that He was going away and they would not be able to follow Him at that time (John 13:36). This declaration of a period of absence bothered the disciples. Christ then calmed their unstable hearts with these warm words:

> Let not your heart be troubled: ye believe in God, believe also in me.
> In my Father's house are many mansions: if it were not so, I would have told you. I go to prepare a place for you.
> And if I go and prepare a place for you, I will come again, and receive you unto myself; that where I am, there ye may be also (John 14:1-3).

Did you catch that? Christ calmed them with a prophetic truth. Comfort came from a promise of a heavenly home and the imminent return of Christ. Would Christ have said something *not* practical at a time like that? Certainly not. When the young Thessalonian believers were sorrowing over the deaths of Christian loved ones, Paul wrote of the return of Jesus Christ, the resurrection of the dead, the translation of the living saints, and the eternal fellowship of the entire group. He concluded, "Wherefore comfort one another with these words" (1 Thess. 4:18). At the time of separation and death, only bright future prospects can calm the troubled, sorrowing heart and mind. Thousands of Christians, even in our generation, can testify to the comfort received from these passages.

Paul also used prophetic truth as an incentive for Christian work and faithfulness. After declaring the mystery of the translation of the Church (1 Cor. 15:51-57) to the Corinthian readers, he exhorted them: "Therefore, my beloved brethren, be ye stedfast, unmoveable, always abounding in the work of the Lord, forasmuch as ye know that your labour is not in vain in the Lord" (1 Cor. 15:58). The fact that Christians could be caught up into Heaven at any moment to receive an incorruptible, immortal body was to be a foundation stone for *present* Christian service. In his second letter to the same church, Paul warned that all Christians one day would give an account to Jesus Christ for their conduct and stewardship (2 Cor. 5:10). Paul, recognizing that he also would be included in that judgment, wrote: "Knowing therefore the terror of the Lord, we persuade men . . ." (2 Cor. 5:11). Paul's evangelistic fervor and passion for the souls of men was in part, at least, based upon the realization that he would have to give an account for his part in the missionary outreach of the church.

When Paul visited the sophisticated, intellectual and idolatrous city of Athens during his second journey, he was invited to address the philosophers on Mars Hill. In his sermon, he declared the identity of the unknown god whom they were ignorantly worshiping. He claimed that the God of the Bible was the One Who had created all things, Who was sustaining all things including the physical life of mankind, and Who would judge all men in the future. He concluded in this way:

> And the times of this ignorance God winked at; but now commandeth all men every where to repent:
> Because he hath appointed a day, in the which he will judge the world in righteousness by that man whom he hath ordained; whereof he hath given assurance unto all men, in that he hath raised him from the dead (Acts 17:30, 31).

To challenge the unsaved to repent of their sins and unbelief, Paul spoke of a future resurrection and judgment, a certainty based upon the physical resurrection of Jesus Christ. Some mocked, but others believed because of this message. When Paul defended his faith in Christ before the Roman procurator Felix and his wife Drusilla, "he reasoned of righteousness, temperance, and judgment to come" (Acts 24:25). This caused Felix to tremble. The prophetic proclamation to "flee the wrath to come" is an integral part of the gospel to the unsaved.

Proof of the authority of the Word of God is directly tied into prophetic utterances: "God, who at sundry times and in divers manners spake in time past unto the fathers by the prophets, Hath in these last days spoken unto us by his Son" (Heb. 1:1, 2). The first Biblical prophet, Moses, became a pattern for all subsequent, God-sanctioned prophets. Late in his life, Moses said: "The LORD thy God will raise up unto thee a Prophet from the midst of thee, of thy brethren, like unto me; unto him ye shall hearken" (Deut. 18:15). The people of Israel responded with a question: "How shall we know the word which the LORD hath not spoken?" (Deut. 18:21). How will we be able to recognize him? How can we distinguish between the false and the true? Moses replied: "When a prophet speaketh in the name of the LORD, if the thing follow not, nor come to pass, that is the thing which the LORD hath not spoken. . ." (Deut. 18:22). The giving of prophecy and the fulfillment of that prophecy were the marks of the genuine prophet. When they had taken place, then the people could heed the contemporary exhortations of the prophet.

The study of prophecy is also necessary for a deep appreciation of the power and wisdom of God. When Isaiah was contending with the idolatrous priests within Israel, he voiced God's words:

> Produce your cause, saith the LORD; bring forth your strong reasons, saith the King of Jacob.
> Let them bring them forth, and shew us what shall happen: let them shew the former things, what they be, that we may consider them, and know the latter end of them; or declare us things for to come.
> Shew the things that are to come hereafter, that we may know that ye are gods: yea, do good, or do evil, that we may be dismayed, and behold it together (Isa. 41:21-23).

Later, Isaiah argued for the uniqueness of God who was able to declare "the end from the beginning, and from ancient times the things that are not yet done, saying, My counsel shall stand, and I will do all my pleasure" (Isa. 46:10). God is omniscient. What He says will come to pass, will take place, because He has the power to control the actions and thoughts of men, both wicked and saintly. God has said: "I have spoken it, I will also bring it to pass; I have purposed it, I will also do it" (Isa. 46:11). God's power and His foreknowledge work together in glorious harmony. Someone has said that prophecy is God's signature upon and within His Book. Only He can accurately predict the future of willful men and nations.

God wants men to understand His purposes, both in the present and in the future. When He was about to destroy Sodom and Gomorrah, He said, "Shall I hide from Abraham that thing which I do" (Gen. 18:17). Revelation of this imminent judgment then caused Abraham to become an intense intercessor in prayer (Gen. 18:23-33). If we know the future doom of lost men, certainly as believers, we should be exercised to pray for their salvation. Throughout the epistles, the apostles warned their readers of the impending danger of apostasy and false teachers within the church (e.g., 1 Tim. 4:1-3; 2 Tim. 3:1-8). Paul even admonished Timothy: "If thou put the brethren in remembrance of these things, thou shalt be a good minister of Jesus Christ" (1 Tim. 4:6). We should understand and proclaim the future purposes of God, both those which stem from His directive decree and those which arise within His permissive will.

Naturally, the study of God's Word should produce a holy life within the Christian. Since "All scripture is given by inspiration of God," it is therefore "profitable for doctrine, for reproof, for correction, for instruction in righteousness: That the man of God may be perfect, throughly furnished unto all good works" (2 Tim. 3:16, 17). This includes the study of prophecy, because prophecy is Scripture; thus such a study *is* profitable for the development of the child of God. After Peter declared that the Day of the Lord would consume the present universe in fire, he wrote: "Seeing then that all these things shall be dissolved, what manner of persons ought ye to be in all holy conversation and godliness" (2 Pet. 3:11). Prophetic study is not merely academic or mental; it is emotional and spiritual. It should draw you closer to Him.

Before we go on, it is imperative to point out that prophetic study is not without its dangers. To many, it is pure novelty. It is a new toy, amusing, entertaining and to be enjoyed for the moment; but when the freshness wears off, it is discarded or forgotten. Let us not be like the Athenians who "spent their time in nothing else, but either to tell, or to hear some new thing" (Acts 17:21). Let us not have "itching ears" and turn unto fables, because we cannot endure sound doctrine (2 Tim. 4:3, 4). Too many Christians run from one prophetic conference to another in order to hear this person's identity of the Antichrist or that preacher's description of the downfall of Russia. They want to hear something new, startling or sensational. If the speaker has no novel interpretation of that passage, then they won't attend the next meeting.

Another danger is that of a spiritual pride. "Knowledge

puffeth up, but charity edifieth" (1 Cor. 8:1). The fact that a person can outline God's plan for the ages, chart the times of the Gentiles from Daniel 2 and 7, or harmonize the seal, trumpet and vial judgments of Revelation does not mean that he is more spiritual or more capable of leadership. Spirituality is based upon one's relationship to the indwelling Holy Spirit. Are you yielded to Him? Is there known sin in your life? A Christian who has had the benefit of prophetic teaching should not "lord it over" young Christians who have not had that opportunity. True knowledge should produce humility and the fruit of the Spirit (Gal. 5:22, 23), not a spiritual caste system. There is no room for "Christian prophetic gnostics" within the church.

Sad to say, many Christians have severed fellowship with one another because of eschatological differences. True Christian fellowship should have its basis in spiritual unity because all believers are in the family of God and are therefore brothers and sisters. The basic doctrine that should unite Christians is the Person and redemptive work of Jesus Christ (1 John 1:3). However, pretribulationists seldom get together with posttribulationists. What fellowship hath amillennialists with premillennialists? Many prophetic enthusiasts fall into the same carnal trap of the Corinthians. They argue: "I am of DeHaan; I am of Walvoord; I am of Barnhouse." What a shame! As important as Biblical prophecy is, it should not separate the brethren. In this study, we must endeavor "to keep the unity of the Spirit in the bond of peace" (Eph. 4:3).

Finally, may we not be accused (along with the Pharisees) of failing to see the Lord Jesus Christ in our study. As we search the Scriptures, may we see that they testify *of Him* (John 5:39). May we not fall at the feet of a human Bible teacher that God is using for our blessing, even as the beloved John on Patmos. Listen to him: "And I fell at his feet to worship him. And he said unto me, See thou do it not: I am thy fellowservant, and of thy brethren that have the testimony of Jesus: worship God: for the testimony of Jesus is the spirit of prophecy" (Rev. 19:10; cf. 22:9). Underscore it again—*Worship God!* Prophecy was intended to point men to Jesus Christ—His Person, His redemptive work, and His coming kingdom. After Jesus announced that the Spirit would show the disciples "things to come," He said: "He [the Holy Spirit] shall glorify me" (John 16:14). May our study do just that!

2 – IS JESUS CHRIST REALLY COMING AGAIN?

IN APOSTOLIC times, there were those who sarcastically asked, "Where is the promise of his coming?" (2 Pet. 3:4). To them, a delay of thirty-five years was enough justification for the denial of Christ's return. The anti-Christian gnostics, who believed that matter was innately evil, actually denied the reality of the first advent. To them it was unthinkable that God, eternal Spirit, could take to Himself a human nature, including a body (1 John 4:3). It required only a simple extension of their logic to deny the physical return of Jesus Christ. Today, 1900 years after our Lord's earthly ministry, there are many within professing Christendom who do not believe in the second coming for the same basic reasons. They argue that if Jesus were really coming again, He would have come by now. Since they deny the miraculous concept of the incarnation, they would naturally reject any thought of a second advent.

Some have argued for a *spiritual* return of Jesus Christ rather than physical. They say that Christ returns to live within the life of a sinner who has been converted. Although it is true that Christ is spiritually present in the believer's life (Gal. 2:20; Col. 1:27), He is still bodily present in the third Heaven. Paul was looking for that "glorious appearing of the great God and our Saviour Jesus Christ" (Titus 2:13), even though Christ was spiritually present in his life. Others state that Christ comes at the death of a Christian to take the soul into paradise or Heaven. Just as the angels carried the spirit of Lazarus into Abraham's bosom before the death and resurrection of Christ (Luke 16:22), so now one is "absent from the body, and to be present with the Lord" (2 Cor. 5:8). However, Paul has stated that the Christian dead will be raised at His second coming (1 Thess. 4:16), and this has hardly taken place. Still others have suggested that Christ came through the advent of the Holy Spirit on the Day of Pentecost (Acts 2). Jesus promised to send the Holy Spirit after His ascension into Heaven. It requires a stretch of imagination to say that Jesus sent Himself. After the Spirit came, Peter preached that the coming of Christ was still future (Acts 3:20).

In the face of these false views, how can the Christian have assurance that Jesus Christ is really coming again? Upon what does he base his hope? It rests upon the authority and integrity of the Biblical record. It has its roots deep within the Old Testament. After the sin and fall of Adam and Eve, God said to Satan in their presence: "And I will put enmity between thee and the woman, and between thy seed and her seed; it shall bruise thy head, and thou shalt bruise his heel" (Gen. 3:15). In this first page of human history, God predicted the advent of His Son, the seed of the woman, who would destroy Satan but who in turn would suffer. This was accomplished on the cross of Calvary.

Throughout His dealings with mankind in general and with Israel in particular, God progressively revealed what the coming redeemer would be like and what He would do. He would be Semitic, a descendant of Noah's son Shem (Gen. 9:26). Coming through the loins of Abraham, Isaac and Jacob, He would be the one in whom "all families of the earth be blessed" (Gen. 12:3; 26:4; 28:14). He would be a king out of the tribe of Judah (Gen. 49:10). His coming would be announced by a star (Num. 24:17; cf. Matt. 2:2). He would be a prophet in the Mosaic tradition (Deut. 18:15, 18). He would also be a priest like unto Samuel (1 Sam. 2:35) but according to the order of Melchizedek (Ps. 110:4; cf. Heb. 5:5, 6). As a descendant of King David, he would be guaranteed a house, throne and an eternal kingdom (2 Sam. 7:16; cf. Luke 1:31-33). He would be called the Anointed One, in fact, the eternal Son of God (Ps. 2:2, 7). For the first time, it was then revealed that He would suffer greatly for the sins of His people (Ps. 22). He would be separated from God, mocked by men, thirsty, pierced in His hands and feet, and gambled over (cf. His cross experience). His entrance into Jerusalem as the King of Glory was predicted (Ps. 24). He was to be virgin born because he would be "God with us" (Isa. 7:14). He was to be both divine and human (Isa. 9:6), Spirit-filled (Isa. 11:2), and preceded by a forerunner (Isa. 40:3). Isaiah graphically described His sufferings on the cross (Isa. 53). He was to be the Son of Man coming with the clouds of Heaven (Dan. 7:13). The time of His coming could actually be determined (Dan. 9:24-27). As the pierced Jehovah, He would one day come to the Mount of Olives, destroy Israel's enemies, and establish a worldwide kingdom of peace and righteousness (Zech. 12:10; 14:4, 9).

The prophets were puzzled over these divine revelations (1 Pet. 1:10, 11). How could the Messiah both suffer and reign? This seemed to be an irreconcilable paradox. It was only after Jesus Christ came that the divine wisdom behind the prophetic declarations was made clear. What the prophets did not see was that it would take two comings to accomplish these things. At His first advent, the Messiah would suffer and die to provide spiritual redemption; at His second coming, He would deliver Israel from her enemies and establish His glorious kingdom. To the Christian, this gives assurance. Just as the prophecies of His first coming were literally fulfilled 1900 years ago, so we can expect that the unfulfilled prophecies of the second coming will literally come to pass.

The Christian also believes that Jesus will come again because He Himself said that He would. This should be enough proof for the obedient disciple of the Master. He is the Son of God; therefore, whatever He has said must come to pass. He was correct when He prophesied the details of His death and resurrection; therefore, His promise to return can be relied upon. Throughout His earthly ministry, He casually talked about the second advent. He did not strain nor force Himself to give eschatological predictions simply because it was expected of Him or because other religious teachers had done so. He did not follow the theology textbook approach either. He did not say: "I have talked to you about God, the Scriptures, man, sin, salvation and angels. Now I must talk to you about the doctrine of last things." Talking about the second advent was like talking about the weather. It was free and natural. He often mentioned this event to His disciples. It was in His parabolic ministry (Luke 12:40). After lamenting the unbelief of Jerusalem, He exclaimed: "Ye shall not see me henceforth, till ye shall say, Blessed is he that cometh in the name of the Lord" (Matt. 23:39). In that verse, He predicted a time of absence, a physical, visible return, and a future reception by Israel. This prompted the disciples to ask for a sign of that coming (Matt. 24:3). So in the Olivet Discourse (Matt. 24, 25), our Lord outlined the conditions that would prevail upon earth prior to His coming and the sign (or signs) of that event. The night before His crucifixion, He assured His disciples with the promise to return (John 14:1-3).

At His illegal trial before Caiaphas and the religious elders of Israel, He answered the question about His deity in this way: "Hereafter shall ye see the Son of man sitting on the right hand of power, and coming in the clouds of heaven" (Matt. 26:64). This caused the Sanhedrin to accuse Him of blasphemy, to sentence Him to death, to spit in His face, and to smite Him (Matt. 26:65-67). Only God could make such a statement, and they rejected His claim to deity. They were right in the former, and wrong in the latter. Why would Jesus have made such an outrageous claim at such a critical time in His life if it were not so? During the forty days of ministry after His resurrection, our Lord again reiterated His original promise. To Peter concerning John, He said: "If I will that he tarry till I come, what is that to thee? follow thou me" (John 21:22). He did not claim His resurrection out from among the dead or His restoration to fellowship with them as the fulfillment of His promise. It was still future. He was going away, this time into the Father's presence; but one day, He would return. Almost sixty years later, our Lord manifested Himself to the last living apostle, John, on the island of Patmos. Again, He promised: "Surely I come quickly" (Rev. 22:20). At different times in different places to different men, our Lord promised to return. The Christian places his confidence and hope in those words.

There is an event in our Lord's life which is often overlooked in a discussion of His return. It is the Transfiguration. John the Baptist, Jesus and the apostles preached the same message throughout Palestine: "Repent ye: for the kingdom of heaven is at hand" (Matt. 3:2; 4:17; 10:7). However, rejection of the message soon led to open hostility and conspiracy to slay Christ. It was at this time that our Lord first mentioned the building of the Church (Matt. 16:18). It was also when our Lord first clearly mentioned His intention to suffer, to be killed, and to rise on the third day (Matt. 16:21). This shocking declaration caused the impetuous Peter to rebuke Him. How could the Christ, the Son of the living God, subject Himself to such shame and disgrace? Peter wanted Him to reign, not to die. It was then that Jesus said:

> For the Son of man shall come in the glory of his Father with his angels; and then he shall reward every man according to his works.
>
> Verily I say unto you, There be some standing here, which shall not taste of death, till they see the Son of man coming in his kingdom (Matt. 16:27, 28).

Unfortunately, in our Bibles there is a chapter break after verse 28. The Transfiguration experience is recorded in Matthew 17:1-13. Look at what Jesus said again. He said some of the disciples would not die before seeing His coming to establish the kingdom that they were anxiously awaiting. But it is a fact that all of them died and that our Lord has not yet come. How can this be? The promise of our Lord (Matt. 16:27, 28) of necessity had to be fulfilled in the Transfiguration experience. Six days later, He took Peter, James and John ("some") into a mountain and was transfigured before them. What happened? What does "transfiguration" mean? When our Lord became man at the incarnation, He emptied Himself of the outward form of deity, the glory that radiated from the beauty of His Person (Phil. 2:5-8). As the divine-human person upon earth, He appeared as any other man. There was no glow radiating from His face, no halo upon His head, and He did not walk two inches above the ground. Only on one occasion did He manifest the essential glory of His Person, and that was the Transfiguration. He permitted the glory of His deity to shine through His flesh and garments. This is the way He will appear when He comes to earth to establish His kingdom. Moses and Elijah, representatives of the Old Testament saints, were also there because these saints will share in the glory of the Messianic Kingdom (Matt. 17:3). Years later, the aged Peter reflected upon that event with these inspired words:

> For we have not followed cunningly devised fables, when we made known unto you the power and coming of our Lord Jesus Christ, but were eyewitnesses of his majesty.
>
> For he received from God the Father honour and glory, when there came such a voice to him from the excellent glory, This is my beloved Son, in whom I am well pleased.
>
> And this voice which came from heaven we heard, when we were with him in the holy mount (2 Pet. 1:16-18).

In the holy mount. Peter now understood the significance of the transfiguration of Jesus Christ. It was a preview of coming events. It was a premature and miniature picture of Christ coming to earth to establish His kingdom in glory, attended by Old Testament saints and witnessed by New Testament believers. Peter was absolutely convinced of the factuality of this event because he had participated in it in a miraculous sort of way. His assurance should bolster our hope and faith.

Angels seem to have a special interest in the return of the Lord. They "desire to look into" the nature of our salvation which will be finalized at the second advent (1 Pet. 1:12). When the Lord Jesus is revealed from Heaven, His "mighty angels" will come to take part in the destruction of the wicked. The voice of the archangel will be heard at that time, and perhaps, an angel will sound the trump of God (1 Thess. 4:16). They have a great share in the outpouring of the divine judgments (seal, trumpet, vial) upon the earth in preparation for the coming of the King of Kings and Lord of Lords (Rev. 6—16). It is no accident then that angels witnessed the ascension of Jesus Christ into Heaven and were the first post-ascension "prophets" of the second advent. They said to the disciples: "Ye men of Galilee, why stand ye gazing up into heaven? this same Jesus, which is taken up from you into heaven, shall so come in like manner as ye have seen him go into heaven" (Acts 1:11). They predicted that Jesus would return to the earth, visibly, bodily and from Heaven. One angel announced His first coming (Luke 1:26-38); two angels declared His second coming. Over 1900 years ago, angels praised God at the birth of Jesus: "Glory to God in the highest, and on earth peace, good will toward men" (Luke 2:14). In the future, they will sing the hallelujah chorus: "The kingdoms of this world are become the kingdoms of our Lord, and of his Christ; and he shall reign for ever and ever" (Rev. 11:15). May we join into the spirit and joy of their certainty.

The apostles definitely believed that Jesus Christ would come again. They preached, taught and wrote about it. It was an indispensable part of their message to the world and to the church. In Peter's second sermon after the descent of the Holy Spirit, he emphasized this fact:

> Repent ye therefore, and be converted, that your sins
> may be blotted out, when the times of refreshing shall come

from the presence of the Lord;
> And he shall send Jesus Christ, which before was
preached unto you (Acts 3:19, 20).

In both of his epistles, Peter wrote of the appearing of Christ
(1 Pet. 1:7, 13; 2 Pet. 1:16). In the first New Testament book ever
written, James exhorted the scattered Jewish Christians: "Be
patient therefore, brethren, unto the coming of the Lord. . . . Be
ye also patient; stablish your hearts: for the coming of the Lord
draweth nigh" (James 5:7, 8). Even at that time, some fifteen
years after our Lord's ascension, there was some anxiety over the
delay of the Lord's return. Paul's writings are saturated with the
truth of the return of Christ and the effects it will have on both
the saved and the unsaved in the world. It would accomplish the
physical and spiritual deliverance of Israel (Rom. 11:26). It would
cause the resurrection of the dead (1 Cor. 15:23), the translation
of living saints (1 Thess. 4:17), and the ultimate change into the
glorious image of Jesus Christ (Phil. 3:20, 21). John echoed this
last concept as being a purifying hope: "Beloved, now are we the
sons of God, and it doth not yet appear what we shall be: but we
know that, when he shall appear, we shall be like him; for we shall
see him as he is" (1 John 3:2, 3). Jude saw the coming of the Lord
as a means of judgment upon the ungodly (Jude 14, 15). Take
away the second advent, and you take away an essential section of
apostolic teaching. They were either right or wrong. If wrong,
then Christ is not coming. If right, and they were, then Christ *is*
coming. May we see the significance of this great event.

When men and women were saved in the first century, they
did not give mental assent to a doctrinal statement or creed.
There were no such creeds in those days. Neither did they put
their trust in a dead Christ, hanging upon a cross, suspended
between Heaven and earth. Paul described the conversion of the
Thessalonians in this way:

> For they themselves shew of us what manner of entering
in we had unto you, and how ye turned to God from idols to
serve the living and true God;
> And to wait for his Son from heaven, whom he raised
from the dead, even Jesus, which delivered us from the wrath
to come (1 Thess. 1:9, 10).

They put their faith in a crucified, buried, resurrected, ascended and coming-again Savior who not only could deliver them from the wrath of Hell and the lake of fire, but also from the impending divine wrath of the Great Tribulation. Theirs was a living hope, both present and future, not just a past experience. If conversions like that took place today, it would revolutionize Christendom and a Christless world.

Down through the nineteen centuries of Christendom, evangelical believers have embraced the fact of Christ's return as one of the great fundamentals of the faith. It was to be maintained, propagated and guarded against all attacks and perversions. During the Roman imperial persecutions of the first three centuries, the martyrs looked up with hope, believing that Christ could come and deliver them from such trials. During the Dark Ages, the belief was maintained by small sects. There was a revival of belief in the Lord's return during the Reformation because hope of deliverance from Catholic persecutions was tied into that event. The great missionary movements in Europe and America were stimulated by an awareness of man's lost condition before God and the shortness of time caused by belief in the nearness of His return. In this century, the great liberal-fundamentalist controversy occurred. What distinguished the two groups was belief in certain doctrines. The fundamentalists believed in the inspiration of Scripture, the virgin birth of Jesus Christ, His essential deity, His substitutionary atonement for sins, His physical resurrection and *the bodily return of Jesus Christ to the earth.* The liberals accepted none of these tenets.

Is Jesus Christ really coming again? With the standing support of the Old Testament prophets, Jesus Christ Himself, the angels, the apostles, former converts and the historical tradition of the church, we answer with a resounding yes. May He come soon is our prayer.

3 – COULD JESUS CHRIST COME TODAY?

WHAT AN EXCITING question! Not, could He come during this century? Nor, could He come in our lifetime? But, is it possible that Jesus Christ could come today—now—at any moment—even while you are reading this book? Is His coming the next prophetic event, or must other prophecies be fulfilled or other events transpire before He can come?

Conservative Bible scholars and theologians are not united in their answers to this question. All are agreed that He is coming again, but they certainly do not agree about the time of the event. They can usually be grouped under three major headings: amillennial, postmillennial, and premillennial. These seem to be difficult, fancy, theological labels, but they are basically simple. The term *millennial* comes from the Latin, meaning "1000 years." This time period is Biblical because John mentioned it six times (Rev. 20:2-7). John saw that during the Millennium Satan would be bound, unable to deceive the nations; that Christ would reign on the earth over the world; that the righteous dead would live and reign with Him at that time; and that the unsaved dead would not be raised until after the Millennium.

The *a*millennialist, therefore, does not believe in a literal, 1000-year reign of Christ on earth (*a* is a negative prefix). He views the language of Revelation as symbolical or allegorical. Although he believes in the personal, visible return of Christ, he denies that Jesus is coming to establish the kingdom of God upon earth. Generally speaking, he also denies the imminency of His return, i.e., that Christ could come at any moment. He suggests that these events must precede His coming: the evangelization of the world, the conversion of an elect remnant within Israel, the great apostasy, and the appearance of signs and wonders.

Postmillennialism was very popular at the turn of the century. It was believed that Christianity would overcome paganism, unbelief and wickedness. Through the evangelistic and social outreach of the church, the world would become Christianized. Once this goal was achieved, then Christ would come and reign over His kingdom. "Bringing in the kingdom" was a catchy phrase in those days. However, two world wars, the Korean and Vietnam conflicts, the depression, the atrocities of the concentration camps and the rapid rise of atheistic communism have smashed the dreams of this view.

Premillennialism teaches that Christ will come to the earth *before (pre)* the establishment of the kingdom. However, not all within this group believe in the imminency of Christ's return. The reason for this difference is the relationship of His return to the great tribulation period, a seven-year age that occurs just before the Millennium. Some premillennialists are also posttribulationists. They believe that Christ will come *after* the tribulation but *before* the Millennium. They believe that the Church will go through the seven-year era and experience the wrath and persecution of the Antichrist. All of the predicted events of the tribulation must first take place before Christ can come. When Christ does come, the dead and the living saints will be caught up to meet Him in the air; then, together they will descend to the earth for the Kingdom Age. He can't come now; that event is at least seven years away.

Others are midtribulationists. They teach that the Church, composed of true believers, will go through the first three and one-half years of tribulation and that Jesus will come in the midst of the period and catch them away into Heaven. Then God will pour out His wrath upon the wicked. At the end of the tribulation, Christ and His saints will return to the earth for His kingdom reign. This view also denies imminency because His coming is at least three and one-half years away.

The only view that can consistently embrace imminency is pretribulational premillennialism. It teaches that Christ can come at any moment to rapture His Church, consisting of all saints, both dead and living, from the Day of Pentecost (Acts 2). Believers will then be in Heaven while the tribulation is taking place on earth. At the end of this period, the Christians will descend with Christ to the earth to share in the blessings of His worldwide kingdom of peace and righteousness. According to this position, there is nothing holding back His return except the divine will and timetable. No prophecy needs to be fulfilled. He could come today.

Serious attention should be given to those arguments that are voiced against imminency, especially as they come from the lips and pens of evangelicals. There are several, but only the most important will be discussed here. The first is based upon our Lord's announcement of Peter's death during His post-resurrection ministry: "When thou wast young, thou girdest thyself, and walkedst whither thou wouldest: but when thou shalt be old, thou shalt stretch forth thy hands, and another shall gird thee, and carry thee whither thou wouldest not. This spake he, signifying by what death he should glorify God" (John 21:18, 19). Peter, late in his life, made reference to this prediction (2 Pet. 1:14, 15). The argument is that Christ could not have come until Peter had become old and had died. This would delay His coming until at least A.D. 65-68, the traditional date of Peter's martyrdom. In reply, Peter was middle-aged at this time because he was neither young nor old (John 21:18). Since the life span was relatively short in those times, he would have been old in just a few years. After Pentecost, Peter faced immediate persecution and possible loss of life several times (Acts 4, 5, 8, 12). His death was actually imminent; therefore, Christ's coming was just as imminent. From our standpoint, this argument no longer has weight. Peter *has* died; thus, that one necessary event is over. Also, these apostles believed that Christ could come and interrupt the natural course of history.

In that connection, the divine and human plans for Paul's ministry are cited as proofs against imminency. Christ commissioned Paul to be a witness unto Gentiles, kings and Israel and to suffer great things (Acts 9:15, 16). Paul had long-distance plans for his missionary journeys (Rom. 15:24). He knew that he would reach Rome (Acts 23:11). Late in life, he even predicted his own death (2 Tim. 4:6). Do not these plans negate a belief in imminency on the part of Paul? Again, it must be said that Paul knew that God could interrupt or change his plans. Paul wanted to go to Bithynia too, but the Holy Spirit stopped him (Acts 16:7). Just because he planned a trip to Spain does not mean that he actually expected to fulfill that ambition. His imprisonments at Caesarea and Rome (total of four years) took precious time away from him. He probably did not get to Spain; the Bible records no such visit. In Paul's mind, the Spirit could stop him again, the Lord's imminent return could interrupt his plans, or imprisonment and/or death could prevent it.

The most popular argument against imminency is based upon the content of the Great Commission. Christ commanded the disciples and the Church to make disciples of all the nations, to go into all the world, and preach the gospel to every creature, and to be witnesses of Him from Jerusalem to the uttermost part of the earth (Mark 16:15; Matt. 28:19; Acts 1:8). Such an extensive program of evangelization would naturally involve a great deal of time and effort; therefore, Christ could not come until the Church had fulfilled her commission. Those who espouse this view admit that any generation which is really dedicated to the task can complete this mission. They thus use it as an incentive for all-out missionary endeavor. *If* we can evangelize the world, then Christ will be able to come in our time.

Although it is true that the present world population has not been completely evangelized, can it be assumed that there was never a generation in which the entire world heard the gospel? Could there ever have been a more dedicated group of missionaries than that of the apostles? Did they not preach extensively throughout the known world of their day? On the Day of Pentecost devout Jews "out of every nation under heaven" heard Peter preach and apparently received Christ (Acts 2:5). If they went back to their respective countries and proclaimed the gospel message, would this not have fulfilled the Great Commission? At Thessalonica, during Paul's first trip into Europe, his adversaries cried: "These that have turned the world upside down are come hither also" (Acts 17:6). At this time, Paul had not yet visited such major cities as Berea, Athens, Corinth or Ephesus. During his first Roman imprisonment (A.D. 62), Paul told the Colossians that the gospel had been "preached to every creature which is under heaven" (Col. 1:23; cf. 1:6). There is good scriptural support for believing that the commission was fulfilled in the apostolic era, possibly very early.

One verse that constantly pops up in this discussion is Matthew 24:14: "And this gospel of the kingdom shall be preached in all the world for a witness unto all nations; and then shall the end come." Spoken during the Olivet Discourse, our Lord was outlining the signs and conditions *in* the tribulation period before His return to the earth *after* the tribulation. During the tribulation, the gospel of the kingdom will be preached again. It is the same message that John the Baptist and Jesus preached: "Repent ye, for the kingdom of heaven is at hand." It will be preached by the two great witnesses (Rev. 11:3), by the 144,000 Jewish evangelists (Rev. 7:4), and by thousands of converted Gentiles (Rev. 7:9). As these are persecuted and scattered by anti-Christian forces, the entire world will hear of the nearness of the Millennial Kingdom. The *end* of the tribulation will then come when Christ returns. This verse does not refer to the preaching of the gospel of the grace of God (1 Cor. 15:3, 4) which is going on today.

It is also pointed out that Jerusalem had to be destroyed before the second advent (Luke 21:20-24). Since the city was not devastated until A.D. 70, He could not have come until then. This position assumes that the destruction had to take place before the rapture of the Church and before the great tribulation period. However, Jesus was talking about His return to the earth. He could have come before A.D. 70, with the destruction taking place during the tribulation. In fact, although it was smashed by the Romans 1900 years ago, it will again be attacked during the future tribulation period. It should also be noted that no one in that day knew when Jerusalem would be destroyed. The Romans were in absolute control of the land when Christ announced His return. Danger to the city was just as imminent as His coming.

In his second Thessalonian epistle Paul had to cope with an eschatological problem:

> Now we beseech you, brethren, by the coming of our Lord Jesus Christ, and by our gathering together unto him,
> That ye be not soon shaken in mind, or be troubled, neither by spirit, nor by word, nor by letter as from us, as that the day of Christ ['day of Lord' in best manuscripts] is at hand.
> Let no man deceive you by any means: for that day shall not come, except there come a falling away first, and that man of sin be revealed, the son of perdition (2 Thess. 2:1-3).

By prophetic utterance, sermon or by a forged Pauline letter, the Thessalonians were told that the tribulations or persecutions they were enduring were those of the great tribulation period. This confused them because Paul taught them earlier that they would not go into the Day of the Lord (1 Thess. 5:1-10). Had they missed out on the rapture for some reason? Those who argue against imminency and pretribulationism state that Paul should have simply pointed out that the rapture had not occurred, if that were the case. However, Paul did mention the rapture (2 Thess. 2:1). He also described what must take place in the Day of the Lord—the apostasy and the manifestation of the Antichrist. Since these were not evident, the Day of the Lord had not started; therefore, their tribulations should not be equated with those of the Great Tribulation. They had not missed out on the rapture. They were right in believing that Christ could come at any moment and deliver them from the pending wrath of the Great Tribulation. What they had been told (2 Thess. 2:2) was in error. They should not be alarmed.

Now let us look at some positive scriptural reasons for accepting the position that Christ could come at any moment. During the Upper Room Discourse given by Jesus to His disciples the night before He was crucified, He said:

> Let not your heart be troubled: ye believe in God, believe also in me.
> In my Father's house are many mansions: if it were not so, I would have told you. I go to prepare a place for you.
> And if I go and prepare a place for you, I will come again, and receive you unto myself; that where I am, there ye may be also (John 14:1-3).

The verb "I will come," according to English grammar, is in the future tense; but in the original Greek text, it is in the present tense. Its transliterated form is *erchomai*. Greek grammarians call it the futuristic usage of the present tense. According to them, it points out an event or action which has not yet taken place, but which is regarded as so certain that in thought it may be regarded as already coming to pass. The verb is also in the indicative mood, the mood of reality rather than of possibility or probability. This is why Christ chose to use the present tense "I *am* coming" in a prophetic situation. He wanted His disciples not to look for Him in the future but rather *in the present*. It was an imminent possibility. Have you ever heard a parent call to his son or daughter, "Will you please come down to breakfast?" Then, the sleepy, half-dressed teenager replies, "I'm coming! I'm coming! Hold your horses!" At that moment, he is using the present tense in a futuristic way. He may not get to the kitchen for ten more minutes, but he has given the impression that he is practically running out of the bedroom and sliding down the banister. This is the impression that Jesus wanted to leave with His disciples. Imminency means that they *could* expect Him at any moment, not that He *would* come in their lifetime.

Most critics of imminency point out that Peter had to die before Christ could come; however, they fail to reveal the fact that the early church believed Christ would come before the death of John the apostle. After our Lord announced the martyrdom of Peter, Peter wondered what would happen to John:

> Then Peter, turning about, seeth the disciple whom Jesus loved following; which also leaned on his breast at supper, and said, Lord, which is he that betrayeth thee?
> Peter seeing him saith to Jesus, Lord, and what shall this man do?
> Jesus saith unto him, If I will that he tarry till I come, what is that to thee? follow thou me.
> Then went this saying abroad among the brethren, that that disciple should not die: yet Jesus said not unto him, He shall not die; but, If I will that he tarry till I come, what is that to thee (John 21:20-23).

The early Christians were mistaken in their dogmatism that John would not die; they were right in thinking that Christ could come in John's lifetime. Notice those words again. Jesus said, "If I will that he tarry till I come. . . ." The translation of John before death was a possibility, but not an absolute certainty, within the divine will. Christ could have willed to come in the first century, but it just was not the appointed time. The fact that Peter was still alive did not detract from their belief in the imminent return of Christ; the fact that John was still alive (especially since he outlived Peter by at least twenty-five years) intensified that faith. Imagine the excitement of the church over the death of Peter and John's escape from that particular persecution. One by one the apostles died, but John lived on. Imagine their increased excitement when Jerusalem was laid waste by the Romans (A.D. 70). Some sources indicate that subsequent to this event, no New Testament book was written for some fifteen years (70-85). Could the human reason be that expectancy of His return was so high that there seemed to be no need for additional revelation? It certainly is a definite possibility. As John lived from one decade to another in that first century, no doubt the Christians were watching his health and looking up into Heaven at the same time.

During his third missionary journey, Paul tried to provoke the Roman church out of their lethargy with these words:

> And that, knowing the time, that now . . . is our salvation nearer than when we believed.
> The night is far spent, the day is at hand: let us therefore cast off the works of darkness, and let us put on the armour of light (Rom. 13:11, 12).

Salvation is threefold (past, present, future), so to what aspect did he refer? It could not refer to the initial deliverance from the penalty of sin because that was past. Paul had already believed in Christ as his personal Savior. It could not refer to progressive salvation or sanctification because this had been and was now taking place in Paul's life. Although physical death in a certain sense delivers a believer from the presence of sin, yet Paul was not anticipating natural death or martyrdom at this time (A.D. 56, 57). This passage must then refer to that final act of salvation, the redemption of the body. Paul had mentioned this truth earlier in the letter: "And not only they, but ourselves also, which have the firstfruits of the Spirit, even we ourselves groan within ourselves, waiting for the adoption, to wit, the redemption of our body" (Rom. 8:23). The body will be redeemed either by resurrection or translation when it is changed into an immortal, incorruptible body, conformed to that glorified, resurrected body of Jesus Christ. This bodily redemption or salvation will occur when Jesus returns. To Paul, this event was imminent or near. Since time was short, these Roman Christians should get busy for the Lord. Paul certainly did not project this event into the distant future.

In the classic Biblical chapter on the resurrection, Paul expressed this hope:

Behold, I shew you a mystery; We shall not all sleep, but
we shall all be changed,

In a moment, in the twinkling of an eye, at the last
trump: for the trumpet shall sound, and the dead shall be
raised incorruptible, and we shall be changed.

For this corruptible must put on incorruption, and this
mortal must put on immortality (1 Cor. 15:51-53).

The resurrection of the dead was no mystery. Old Testament
saints fully expected to be raised in the last day (Job 19:25-27; Isa.
26:19; Dan. 12:2, 3). Concerning Lazarus, even Martha said, "I
know that he shall rise again in the resurrection at the last day"
(John 11:24). What then was the mystery? It was that believers
could suddenly be caught up into the presence of God to receive
an immortal, incorruptible body apart from physical death. It is
true that Enoch and Elijah went into Heaven apart from death,
but these were the rare exceptions. Nowhere in the Old
Testament did other believers expect this to happen to them. This
truth was first revealed after the Lord's death and resurrection.
Paul himself believed that Christ could come in his lifetime—in
fact, at any moment. See how he used the word *we* in this passage.
Christ did not come in Paul's generation, but He could have. It is
very possible that our Lord could come in our generation, even
today. If He does, then all living believers will cheat death and the
undertaker.

Paul commended the Thessalonian Christians for patiently
waiting for Jesus who "delivered us from the wrath to come" (1
Thess. 1:10). At first glance, it appears that Paul is talking about
the deliverance from the penalty of sin (Hell, lake of fire, wrath of
God) that comes through receiving Christ as Savior. However, this
is not the case. A literal translation of this phrase is: "Jesus, the
one who *is delivering* us out of the wrath, the *coming one.*" Both the
italicized verbal forms are present participles, used in the
futuristic sense again (cf. John 14:3). This is not a past
deliverance; this is the possibility of a *present* deliverance from a
wrath which could come at any moment. The wrath of God
presently abides upon the unbeliever (John 3:36); the Christian
has always been saved from that (John 5:24). What wrath then is
coming, imminent? It is the wrath of God to be manifested in the
great tribulation period. Later, in another eschatological passage,

Paul wrote: "For God hath not appointed us to wrath, but to obtain salvation by our Lord Jesus Christ" (1 Thess. 5:9). This coming wrath is just as imminent as the delivering return of Jesus Christ. By turning to God from idols, the Thessalonians had been saved from the wrath of God, the penalty of sin; now, they were expectantly waiting for Christ to return from Heaven to take them into Heaven in order to escape the wrath of God to be poured out in the tribulation (Rev. 6—16).

James exhorted his readers to be patient unto the coming of the Lord. He said that His coming had drawn near and that He, the Judge, was standing before the door (James 5:7-9). This is an interesting metaphor. Christ has taken up His position outside the door to earth. He has raised His hand. He is just about to knock and to open the door. Who knows when His hand will hit the door and we will be ushered into His presence? This is why James told them to "grudge not one against another." If you knew that the pastor was going to visit your house, would you and your family be arguing at that time? Certainly not. Wouldn't it be ridiculous to be caught up into the presence of God while arguing over the kitchen table or in a church business meeting? There is no telephone warning before His coming either.

The beloved John said this about His return: "And now, little children, abide in him; that, when he shall appear, we may have confidence, and not be ashamed before him at his coming" (1 John 2:28). The phrase, "when he shall appear," also repeated later (3:2), is literally translated "if he shall be manifested." The subjunctive mood, the mood of probability, is used with the conditional "if." John certainly was not wondering whether Christ might appear; that was a fact, not a probability. What was uncertain was the *time* of His coming. No one knows *when* that will take place, not even the angels in Heaven (Matt. 24:36). It could be today; it could be tomorrow; and it could be one hundred years away. Who knows for sure? This is what John wanted to communicate. Christ can be expected at any time.

The closing prophecy and prayer in the Bible reads: "He which testifieth these things saith, Surely, I come quickly. Amen. Even so, come, Lord Jesus" (Rev. 22:20). Christ again used the futuristic present tense which emphasizes the imminency of the event (cf. John 14:3). He said that His return would not only be speedy ("in the twinkling of an eye") but also imminent.

Remember that God does not reckon time as we do (2 Pet. 3:8). To Him, a thousand years is as one day. And yet, the believer, even as John, should pray every day, "Even so, come, Lord Jesus." May it be today!

As we have seen, the Bible definitely teaches that the return of Christ for His own is imminent. In a sense, it is not correct to say that He is coming soon. Our concept of His appearing should be the same as that of the Biblical authors and of the early church. If His coming is *soon,* then they were mistaken, because two thousand years have elapsed. At Thanksgiving time, you could say that Christmas is coming soon, but you could not say that it is imminent. This difference should also be applied to His return.

What then should be our attitude as Christians toward this great event in His life and in ours? First, it should create in us a quality of patient expectation. Just as the farmer "waiteth for the precious fruit of the earth, and hath long patience for it, until he receive the early and latter rain" (James 5:7), so we should wait patiently for Him. As mentioned before, the Thessalonians "turned to God from idols to serve the living and true God; And to wait for his Son from heaven" (1 Thess. 1:9, 10). They manifested a spiritual triad for which Paul commended them and others: the work of faith, the labor of love, and the patience of hope (1 Thess. 1:3). Even the carnal Corinthians who lacked in no gift were "waiting for the coming of our Lord Jesus Christ" (1 Cor. 1:7). Don't become anxious or apprehensive. Wait, because one day faith will become sight.

"Watch therefore, for ye know neither the day nor the hour wherein the Son of man cometh" (Matt. 25:13). Jesus said that His disciples (we, too) should be sober and alert, watching and looking for Him. As they watched Him go into Heaven (Acts 1:9) with their physical eyes, so their spiritual eyes should be looking up and focused in order to catch that first glimpse of Him. Paul told Titus that the grace of God is a teacher:

> For the grace of God that bringeth salvation hath appeared to all men,
> Teaching us that, denying ungodliness and worldly lusts, we should live soberly, righteously, and godly, in this present world;
> Looking for that blessed hope, and the glorious

appearing of the great God and our Saviour Jesus Christ (Titus 2:11-13).

Looking for Him will cause you to *live* for Him. If you are living for Him, then you will be looking for Him. They go together.

In that connection, John wrote:

> Beloved, now are we the sons of God, and it doth not yet appear what we shall be: but we know that, when he shall appear, we shall be like him; for we shall see him as he is.
>
> And every man that hath this hope in him purifieth himself, even as he is pure (1 John 3:2, 3).

A living hope is a purifying hope. If we *really* believed that Christ could come today, our lives would be radically changed. We would be living "soberly, righteously, and godly, in this present world" (Titus 2:12). Think about it. Would you want Him to find you playing with that secret sin if He should come today? Our Heavenly Bridegroom one day is going to present His Bride, the Church, to His Father, "not having spot, or wrinkle, or any such thing; but that it should be holy and without blemish" (Eph. 5:27). If we love our spiritual fiancée, then we should be bridal white and pure for Him. May He not catch us "having a spiritual affair" with the world. Otherwise, we would certainly be ashamed at His coming. "Therefore be ye also ready: for in such an hour as ye think not the Son of man cometh" (Matt. 24:44). Take a tip from the Boy Scouts: Be prepared!

The hope of His return should produce comfort within the life of the believer by the Holy Spirit. At the death of a Christian loved one, we should have sorrow but not as "others which have no hope" (1 Thess. 4:13). Even Jesus wept at the tomb of Lazarus just before He manifested His resurrection power (John 11:35). When standing at the deathbed or the funeral casket, the Christian should realize that the departed believer is "absent from the body, and . . . present with the Lord" (2 Cor. 5:8). One day they will see each other again, nevermore to be separated. "Wherefore comfort one another with these words" (1 Thess. 4:18).

Belief in the imminent return of Christ should produce faithful, enthusiastic work for the Lord. Paul wrote: "Therefore, my beloved brethren, be ye stedfast, unmoveable, always abounding in the work of the Lord, forasmuch as ye know that your labour is not in vain in the Lord" (1 Cor. 15:58). Who knows how much more time we will have to serve Him? Let us be busy in the work of the Master.

> Who then is a faithful and wise servant, whom his lord hath made ruler over his household, to give them meat in due season?
> Blessed is that servant, whom his lord when he cometh shall find so doing (Matt. 24:45, 46).

This story is told about three fishermen, a father and his two married sons. After laboring all night harvesting the sea in their family boat, they began to return home. On the way back, they were discussing their wives. The first son said that he knew what his wife would be doing at the early morning hour. She would be *waiting* for him, sitting in the rocking chair by the open fire. The second son said that his wife also would be up, but in addition, she would be at the window, *watching* for his shadowy form to come up the lane. The father then smiled and said, "Your mother, my wife, also will be waiting and watching for me, but she will be busy *working* in the kitchen. She wants to greet her beloved husband with hot coffee and a warm breakfast besides a loving kiss." Let us also be waiting, watching and working for Him.

4 – WHAT IS THE BLESSED HOPE
OF THE CHURCH?

ONE OF THE MOST beautiful words in all of the English language is *hope*. The young woman hoards silverware and china in her hope chest, looking forward to engagement and marriage. A family hangs on to words of hope from the doctor's mouth as a loved one goes into surgery. Children hope for those special Christmas gifts.

Hope is also one of the basic Christian words, comparable to faith and love (1 Cor. 13:13). Paul said that "we are saved by hope: but hope that is seen is not hope: for what a man seeth, why doth he yet hope for? But if we hope for that we see not, then do we with patience wait for it" (Rom. 8:24, 25). The sensitive child of God is especially "looking for that blessed hope, and the glorious appearing of the great God and our Saviour Jesus Christ" (Titus 2:13). The coming of Christ for His own, therefore, is the blessed hope of the Church.

In order to understand this more fully, we need to know what the Church is. After our Lord was rejected by His own nation, He announced, "I will build my church; and the gates of hell shall not prevail against it" (Matt. 16:18). He went on to say that the Church would be built upon the foundation of His suffering death and resurrection (Matt. 16:21). Paul, by the Spirit of God, equated the Church with the Body of Christ, over which He is the Head (Eph. 1:22, 23). It had been planned by God the Father, paid for by God the Son, and is presently protected by God the Holy Spirit (Eph. 1:3-14). It is composed of sinful men who have become saints, dead men who have come alive by the grace of God (Eph. 2:1-10). To form the Church, God not only removed the sin barrier between man and Himself, but He also broke down the racial barrier that existed between Jew and Gentile (Eph. 2:11-20). Both converted Jews and Gentiles are one in the Body of Christ. It exists as the habitation of the Spirit in order to manifest the glory of God and the manifold wisdom of God (Eph. 1:14; 3:10).

The Church is a mystery. It did not exist nor was it expected in the Old Testament period. It was predicted that Gentiles would be saved and that they would enter into the blessings of the Jewish kingdom, however the racial distinction would continue. It was nowhere revealed that Gentiles would be one with Jews and "fellowheirs, and of the same body, and partakers of his promise in Christ by the gospel" (Eph. 3:6).

How does one get into the Body of Christ? The only passage that describes the means is 1 Corinthians 12:13: "For by [in] one Spirit are we all baptized into one body, whether we be Jews or Gentiles, whether we be bond or free; and have been all made to drink into one Spirit." During our Lord's post-resurrection ministry to the apostles, He predicted that they would be baptized in the Holy Spirit in a few days (Acts 1:5). Ten days after His ascension, the Holy Spirit descended and "filled all the house where they were sitting" (Acts 2:2). They were literally enveloped, immersed and baptized *in* the Spirit. The Day of Pentecost, then, was the birthday of the Church, the beginning of a new age or dispensation. God was doing a new thing. He formerly (for 2000 years) dealt with the world through Israel, His covenant nation; now He would work through the Church. This distinctive period will end when the Body of Christ is fully matured, when the last living cell has been produced, when the last sinner has been saved in this era (Eph. 4:12, 13). Then, Christ will come and catch His own into Heaven. Then, the living Head and the living Body will truly be one, not only spiritually and organically, but also geographically. Who knows at what stage in the maturing process of the Body of Christ we are in today? The blessed hope, consequently, was not the hope of the Old Testament or gospel periods; it is uniquely *our* hope, the hope of all believers from the Day of Pentecost to this present day.

The classic passage that deals with this hope is found in Paul's first letter to the Thessalonian church, written from Corinth during his second missionary journey:

> But I would not have you to be ignorant, brethren, concerning them which are asleep, that ye sorrow not, even as others which have no hope.
> For if we believe that Jesus died and rose again, even so

them also which sleep in Jesus will God bring with him.

For this we say unto you by the word of the Lord, that we which are alive and remain unto the coming of the Lord shall not prevent them which are asleep.

For the Lord himself shall descend from heaven with a shout, with the voice of the archangel, and with the trump of God: and the dead in Christ shall rise first:

Then we which are alive and remain shall be caught up together with them in the clouds to meet the Lord in the air: and so shall we ever be with the Lord.

Wherefore comfort one another with these words (1 Thess. 4:13-18).

In his synagogue ministry at Thessalonica, Paul reasoned out of the Old Testament that the promised Messiah had to die and to rise out of the grave and that Jesus of Nazareth was indeed that Messiah (Acts 17:1-9). Many of the Jews and Greek proselytes believed his message. In addition, many pagan idolaters were converted to Christ (1 Thess. 1:9). This successful ministry incurred the wrath and persecution of the jealous, unbelieving Jews to such an extent that Paul was forced to leave the city. The young Thessalonian Christians were left behind with the living hope that Jesus could come at any moment and deliver them from their tribulations. Jesus didn't come, and some of them had died either by natural causes or by persecution. They were troubled. Would their departed loved ones miss out on the blessings of the blessed hope? When Paul heard about their perplexity, he wrote the above passage to them. He did not want them to be ignorant about the relationship of the Christian dead to the return of Jesus Christ (1 Thess. 4:13).

First of all, he told them that their sorrow should not be of the same type as that of non-Christians. As emotional, loving beings, we should feel a sense of loss when a close friend or relative dies; however, we have *hope*. There is life beyond death! Death is not the end, a leap into oblivion or darkness. Our Savior has "abolished death, and hath brought life and immortality to light through the gospel" (2 Tim. 1:10). To the Christian, death simply ushers one from this life into the eternal presence of God. Paul said that "to live is Christ, and to die is gain" (Phil. 1:21). The dying one goes "to be with Christ; which is far better" (Phil. 1:23). When a believer dies, he is "absent from the body, and . . . present with the Lord" (2 Cor. 5:8). The body may be in the ground, but the real "you," the personality (intellect, emotion, will), the soul, the immaterial part of human life, is in Heaven. Earth's loss, then, is Heaven's gain. This is why the psalmist cried: "Precious in the sight of the LORD is the death of his saints" (Ps. 116:15). The little child's prayer is very close to this Biblical idea:

> Now I lay me down to sleep, I pray the Lord my soul to keep;
> And if I die before I wake, I pray the Lord my soul to take.

As far as the body is concerned, Paul says that it is "asleep." This implies a time of waking up in the resurrection morning. The psalmist prayed: "As for me, I will behold thy face in righteousness: I shall be satisfied, when I awake, with thy likeness" (Ps. 17:15). Thus, the child of God can have tears in his eyes and joy in his heart as he views the lifeless form of a Christian loved one.

There was a time (*before* Christ's death, resurrection and ascension) when the departed spirits of all men, both saved and unsaved, went into Hades, which means "the unseen place" (Luke 16:19-31). On the cross, Jesus said to the repentant thief: "To day shalt thou be with me in paradise" (Luke 23:43). Since the spirit of our Lord went into Hades (or Hell) at His death (Acts 2:27), then paradise and Abraham's bosom, where the beggar Lazarus was comforted, must be the same. Hades, then, was divided into two sections—a place of torment and a place of comfort. However, when Jesus ascended into Heaven, He took with Him the spirits of the Old Testament saints (Eph. 4:8-10). So today, paradise must be equated with the third Heaven (2 Cor. 12:2, 4). The Christian goes there upon death; the unsaved still go to the place of torment in Hades.

In 1 Thessalonians 4:14, Paul based the blessed hope upon faith in the death and resurrection of Jesus Christ. Without the historical fact of His bodily resurrection, there would be no future resurrection of the dead. If He was not raised, then our message and faith are without content and useless (1 Cor. 15:12-19). This would mean that we have put our faith in a dead Christ, and a dead Christ can't save anyone. Pity those who have already died, clinging to this hope. "But now is Christ risen from the dead, and become the firstfruits of them that slept" (1 Cor. 15:20). His resurrection from the tomb guarantees the resurrection of all believers. It is an essential part of the gospel message (1 Cor. 15:3, 4). A man cannot become a Christian apart from faith in the risen Lord: "That if thou shalt confess with thy mouth the Lord Jesus, and shalt believe in thine heart that God hath raised him from the dead, thou shalt be saved" (Rom. 10:9). Truly, He "was delivered for our offences, and was raised again for our justification" (Rom. 4:25). Only if a person has such faith can he have the hope of this passage.

How will those who are in Heaven be able to be caught up to meet the Lord? They are already there. This is what puzzled the Thessalonians. Paul said that "them also which sleep in Jesus will God bring with him" (1 Thess. 4:14). When our Lord begins to descend from Heaven, the spirits of the departed Christian dead will accompany Him. These spirits will be sent on ahead to be united to their resurrection bodies. Then the complete person, in a new body, will be raised from the dead to "ground" level. United with the living saints in one body, they will be caught up *together* to meet the Lord in the air. This means that the living Christian will have no advantage over the one who has died. He will not see the Lord first in an immortal, incorruptible body. The old English word *prevent* today means "precede." The living saint will *not* precede or go on ahead of the Christian dead. They will meet the Lord simultaneously.

At that time, living Christians will truly enter into the mystery of the rapture. When "we which are alive and remain unto the coming of the Lord" are caught up to meet the Lord (1 Thess. 4:15, 17), the mystery feature will be fulfilled. Paul wrote:

> Behold, I shew you a mystery; We shall not all sleep, but we shall all be changed,
> In a moment, in the twinkling of an eye, at the last trump: for the trumpet shall sound, and the dead shall be raised incorruptible, and we shall be changed (1 Cor. 15:51, 52).

Part of the blessing of the blessed hope is that our Lord could come today and we believers would immediately be translated into His presence.

> O joy! O delight! should we go without dying,
> No sickness, no sadness, no dread and no crying,
> Caught up through the clouds with our Lord into glory,
> When Jesus receives His own.

Just as Enoch and Elijah long ago, we could ascend into Heaven "in a moment, in the twinkling of an eye." Not in the time that it takes to *blink* the eye, but in the *twinkle* of an eye. Before you can say "He's here," it's over! Should not our song and prayer be:

> O Lord Jesus, how long, how long
> Ere we shout the glad song—
> Christ returneth! Hallelujah!
> Hallelujah! Amen, Hallelujah! Amen.

The fact that "the Lord himself shall descend" is a precious truth to the child of God. He is not going to send Michael or Gabriel or some other angel to bring us into Heaven; He is coming *Himself*. When foreign dignitaries visit our country, they are often greeted at the Washington airport by the vice-president, by the secretary of state or by some other cabinet member. But when the president goes from the White House to meet this ambassador or head of state, then you know that the visitor is *very* important. Our Lord is going to receive us personally. Why? Because we *are* important to Him and because He loves us.

Everyone is curious about the resurrection body. What will it be like? Will the ten-year-old boy have a childish body? What about the Christian who dies at eighty? Will he have an old body or a middle-aged one? What about infants who die? Will we be able to recognize one another? How? Even first-century Christians wondered about these things:

> But some man will say, How are the dead raised up? and with what body do they come?
> Thou fool, that which thou sowest is not quickened, except it die:
> And that which thou sowest, thou sowest not that body that shall be, but bare grain, it may chance of wheat, or of some other grain:

But God giveth it a body as it hath pleased him, and to every seed his own body (1 Cor. 15:35-38).

Paul said that the resurrection body will be related to and based upon the natural body, just as the stalk of grain is related to the sown seed. However, it is not identical to the natural body. The natural body was mortal (subject to death) and corruptible (subject to disease and decay). The resurrection body will never die nor be weakened by sickness. The earthly body is a "flesh and blood" body, and that type is not able to "inherit the kingdom of God" (1 Cor. 15:50). The spiritual body will have flesh and bone, but it will not have blood. When Jesus first appeared to His disciples after His resurrection, they thought that He was a ghost, a phantom, a spirit. He said: "Why are ye troubled? and why do thoughts arise in your hearts? Behold my hands and my feet, that it is I myself: handle me, and see; for a spirit hath not flesh and bones, as ye see me have" (Luke 24:38, 39). Since "we shall be like him; for we shall see him as he is" (1 John 3:2), we likewise will have material bodies: bodies that can be seen and touched, bodies that can speak, bodies that can eat, bodies that can go through solid substances (e.g., Christ walked through a closed door), and bodies that will never die. Many questions about the character of the resurrection body cannot be answered, simply because God has chosen not to reveal the information. Someone once said that the Bible was not written to satisfy our curiosity, but to teach us how to live. God is going to give us a body as it pleases Him (1 Cor. 15:38), and that should be good enough for all of us.

After the resurrection and the rapture, what will life be like? How will we live in Heaven? It was this kind of question that the Sadducees asked our Lord in order to trick Him. No doubt they had asked their ancient enemies, the Pharisees, this same question, and had never received an adequate answer; so now they were going to try it out on Jesus. The Sadducees, greatly influenced by Greek philosophy, did not believe in the resurrection of the dead and denied the existence of the spirit and of angels (Acts 23:8). They put forth this hypothetical problem: A woman was married to seven different men; "in the resurrection whose wife shall she be of the seven? for they all had her" (Matt. 22:28). Would she be married to her first husband? Last? Youngest? Oldest? Best? Worst? None? All? Christ did not directly answer this question. Instead, He rebuked them for their denial of life beyond death. The Old Testament taught the resurrection, and certainly God is powerful enough to raise the dead (Matt. 22:29). If He could take the dust of the ground, breathe into it, and create Adam, certainly He could quicken a lifeless corpse. He then remarked: "For in the resurrection they neither marry, nor are given in marriage, but are as the angels of God in heaven" (Matt. 22:30). From this verse, some have derived the idea that we will be sexless in Heaven, even as the angels. However, this is not what Jesus taught. He simply stated that resurrection is not a restoration to natural, human relationships. On earth men and women have to live together in family units to continue the race; however, there will be no need for that in Heaven. We will not live in Heaven as husband and wife or parents with children. Angels exist in Heaven to serve and to worship God; so will we.

Before we leave the nature of the blessed hope, the bearing of progressive revelation in the Scriptures upon Christ's return should be observed. When the ancient prophets spoke of the coming of the Messiah-Redeemer, they saw only *one* coming. Time and further revelation showed that there were two comings: the first to suffer and the second to reign. When our Lord spoke of His second advent, the disciples looked forward to a *single* event. Again, time and more revelation manifested that His second coming would have two stages or phases. He would first come before the tribulation period *for* His own; this is the blessed hope. Then, He would come *after* the tribulation *with* His own to the earth to establish His kingdom. This latter coming, announced by signs, will be discussed in a later chapter.

The blessed hope holds many personal blessings for the child of God. First and foremost, it will effect the reunion and union of the redeemed with the Savior. The Bible does not describe the future of the Christian as being in Heaven, but rather with Christ. Jesus promised: "I will come again, and receive you unto myself; that where I am, there ye may be also" (John 14:3). Paul wrote that after we meet the Lord in the air, "so shall we ever be with the Lord" (1 Thess. 4:17). It is true that we will be in Heaven with Him, but when He comes to rule over the Millennial Kingdom on earth, we will come and reign with Him. To the disciples and others who walked with Him 1900 years ago, it will be a wonderful time of reunion. But what about us? We have never looked upon His face before. What Jesus said to doubting Thomas can also be applied to us: "Thomas, because thou hast seen me, thou hast believed: blessed are they that have not seen, and yet have believed" (John 20:29). Faith will become sight when we catch that first glimpse of Him. Christians, with great anticipation, should be able to sing along with blind Fanny Crosby these glorious words:

> Through the gates to the city, in a robe of spotless white
> He will lead me where no tears will ever fall;
> In the glad song of ages I shall mingle with delight—
> But I long to meet my Savior first of all.
>
> I shall know Him, I shall know Him,
> And redeemed by His side I shall stand,
> I shall know Him, I shall know Him
> By the print of the nails in His hand.

At this time, the believer will also share in His glory. "When Christ, who is our life, shall appear, then shall ye also appear with him in glory" (Col. 3:4). Not only will we view His glorious appearing (Titus 2:13), but we will be brought into glory as the sons of God (Heb. 2:10). The Lord's prayer will then be answered: "Father, I will that they also, whom thou hast given me, be with me where I am; that they may behold my glory, which thou hast given me: for thou lovedst me before the foundation of the world" (John 17:24). With Him forever! What a glorious future!

The coming of Christ will also produce the reunion between loved ones: husband with wife, mother with son, brother with sister. At the resurrection and translation, we will be united to meet the Lord, nevermore to be separated by death or by geography. Paul also looked upon this event as a time of reunion with those he had won to the Lord: "For what is our hope, or joy, or crown of rejoicing? Are not even ye in the presence of our Lord Jesus Christ at his coming? For ye are our glory and joy" (1 Thess. 2:19, 20). Because of persecution, Paul had been taken from his beloved Thessalonians "in presence, not in heart" (1 Thess. 2:17). He was hindered by Satan from revisiting them, so he was anticipating that reunion that no adversary could stop. Wouldn't it be wonderful if we could look forward to seeing some spiritual children then?

His return will also mark the completion of our personal salvation. Our mortal, corruptible bodies groan for release from the physical effects of sin. They want to be redeemed (Rom. 8:23). Only then can the Christian shout the victory song:

> So when this corruptible shall have put on incorruption, and this mortal shall have put on immortality, then shall be brought to pass the saying that is written, Death is swallowed up in victory.
>
> O death, where is thy sting? O grave, where is thy victory?
>
> The sting of death is sin; and the strength of sin is the law.
>
> But thanks be to God, which giveth us the victory through our Lord Jesus Christ (1 Cor. 15:54-57).

When our vile bodies have been "fashioned like unto his glorious body" (Phil. 3:21), then God's eternal decree, His personal plan for each of us, will be consummated. He has predestinated us "to be conformed to the image of his Son," and He will not rest until He has glorified all those whom He has predestinated, called, justified, and loved (Rom. 8:28-30). Then "we shall be like him; for we shall see him as he is" (1 John 3:2). What a blessed hope! Deliverance from the total presence of sin! No more sickness, death, mental illness, deformity—no more sin!

We will then be a suitable Bride (wife) for the sinless Bridegroom. We then can be presented as a "glorious church, not having spot, or wrinkle, or any such thing; but that it should be holy and without blemish" (Eph. 5:27). Since that is our future, should not our present Christian experience be holy? Should not our practice match our prospect? For this Paul prayed: "And the very God of peace sanctify you wholly; and I pray God your whole spirit and soul and body be preserved blameless unto the coming of our Lord Jesus Christ" (1 Thess. 5:23). Pure then—why not now?

As the children of God, we are heirs of God and joint heirs with Jesus Christ (Rom. 8:17); but we have not received that inheritance yet. Peter said that is "incorruptible, and undefiled, and that fadeth not away, reserved in heaven for you" (1 Pet. 1:4). When we get to Heaven, then we will be able to enjoy it.

Deliverance from the wrath of the Great Tribulation is also a blessing (1 Thess. 1:10; 5:9). We are children of the light and of the day, not of darkness or of the night. Our character and destiny are foreign to that of the Day of the Lord (1 Thess. 5:1-5). The posttribulationist argues that as Israel was preserved on earth when the plagues of God fell upon Egypt, so the Church will not be removed from the presence of the tribulation, but it will be preserved and delivered in and through that period. But light and darkness cannot coexist. God is not only going to rapture us before the wrath of the tribulation is poured out, but He is also going to keep us from the very *hour* of the period. Concerning the true Church, Jesus said: "I also will keep thee from the hour of temptation, which shall come upon all the world, to try them that dwell upon the earth" (Rev. 3:10). We will be delivered from both the wrath of God and the wrath of the Antichrist. It could be today. "But let us, who are of the day, be sober, putting on the breastplate of faith and love; and for an helmet, the hope of salvation" (1 Thess. 5:8). That hope is the blessed hope—salvation from the Great Tribulation.

5 – WHAT IS THE GREAT TRIBULATION PERIOD?

THROUGHOUT history there have been times of unusual hatred and persecution of minority groups. The Egyptians, led by their Pharaoh, tried to exterminate all male babies born to Jewish families in the time of Moses (Exod. 1). Haman's plot to destroy all of the Jews within the Persian Empire was providentially overruled through the intervention of Esther and Mordecai. The jealous Herod the Great, enraged by the report of the birth of the Messiah, issued a decree to slay all male infants, two years and under, in the territory involving Bethlehem (Matt. 2). The early Christian church survived many Roman imperial persecutions as thousands of martyrs were burned at the stake or fed to the lions. During the Dark Ages, even the established church oppressed the minority sects with its infamous inquisitions. The most recent case of human atrocities has come out of World War II in anti-Semitic, Nazi Germany where six million Jews were gassed, burned and experimented upon as guinea pigs. It doesn't seem possible that anything could top this, but Jesus predicted:

> Then let them which be in Judaea flee into the mountains:
> Let him which is on the housetop not come down to take any thing out of his house:
> Neither let him which is in the field return back to take his clothes.
> And woe unto them that are with child, and to them that give suck in those days!
> But pray ye that your flight be not in the winter, neither on the sabbath day:
> For then shall be great tribulation, such as was not since the beginning of the world to this time, no, nor ever shall be (Matt. 24:16-21).

The period of Hitler and Eichmann *will* be surpassed. Somewhere in the future, there will be an unparalleled, unprecedented time of trouble that will cause all other such periods to sink into oblivion and forgetfulness. Jesus Christ called it *the Great Tribulation.*

The tribulation was first mentioned by Moses in his closing remarks to the nation of Israel shortly before his death and their subsequent entrance into Canaan. He admonished them to repent and to be obedient "when thou art in tribulation, and all these things are come upon thee, even in the latter days" (Deut. 4:30). The significance of this passage is the fact that Israel had not yet possessed the Promised Land. Times of glory and power under David and Solomon were still future; and yet Moses, by the Spirit of God, looked beyond to a time of tribulation in *the latter days* of Israel's history. The Babylonian captivity (605-536 B.C.) and the Roman dispersion (A.D. 70) certainly do not satisfy the latter day destiny of Israel.

The prophets described it as a time of wrath, judgment, indignation, trial, trouble, destruction, darkness, desolation, overturning and punishment (Isa. 2:19; 24:1, 3, 6, 19-21; 26:20, 21; Joel 1:15; 2:2, 31, 32). Zephaniah aptly denoted it this way:

> The great day of the LORD is near, it is near, and hasteth greatly, even the voice of the day of the LORD: the mighty man shall cry there bitterly.
> That day is a day of wrath, a day of trouble and distress, a day of wasteness and desolation, a day of darkness and gloominess, a day of clouds and thick darkness (Zeph. 1:14, 15).

Jeremiah called it "the time of Jacob's trouble" (Jer. 30:7). He said that there was no day like it, but that Israel would be delivered through it. Daniel likewise stated that it was "a time of trouble, such as never was since there was a nation even to that same time" (Dan. 12:1). In Revelation, the New Testament complement of Daniel, it is "the hour of temptation, which shall come upon all the world, to try them that dwell upon the earth" (3:10). The wicked of the tribulation call it the great day of the wrath of the Lamb of God (Rev. 6:16, 17).

As one views these passages, it is definitely erroneous to

believe and to predict that prosperity is just around the corner, and that the world will get better and better. The future still holds the darkest page of human history. The Christian can still be optimistic, however, because he can see through the dark clouds of the Great Tribulation to the sunshine and silver lining of the Millennial Kingdom, a time of glory, peace and righteousness (to be discussed later).

After the Church Age is terminated by the rapture, the next unique time period in which God will work out His eternal program will be the Great Tribulation. Some have hesitated to call it a separate dispensation or age; they see it as an extension of the law dispensation or simply as an interval between the age of grace (church) and the Millennial Kingdom. All would have to admit, however, that there are distinctive features within the tribulation that are not found in any other age.

A study of the Scriptures will show that God is working out His divine purpose through distinguishable economies, marked off by beginnings and endings. The first, called the dispensation of innocence, began with the creation of Adam and ended with his expulsion from the Garden of Eden. The second, called conscience, began after the fall of man and was climaxed by the catastrophic, universal flood of Noah's time. The third, the age of human government, started with the Noahic Covenant and ended with the multiplication of tongues at the tower of Babel. The fourth, the patriarchal dispensation of promise, began with the divine promises given to Abraham and ended with the nation of Israel in Egyptian bondage. The age of law, the fifth, began with the Exodus and was consummated by the advent and the rejection of the Messiah, Jesus Christ. The Church Age, the sixth, began with the descent of the Holy Spirit on the Day of Pentecost and will end with the rapture, or Christ's coming *for* His own. We are *now* in the Church Age. The Great Tribulation will follow. After that, the seventh age, the Millennial Kingdom (1000-year rule of Christ), will be ushered in by the return of Christ to the earth and will end in the Satanic rebellion, climaxed in the Great White Throne Judgment. After this event, God will introduce the eternal state with the new heavens and the new earth.

At this point, we must distinguish between the Great Tribulation, a future time period, and tribulations which we Christians are expected to receive and to endure in this life. Jesus said: "In the world ye shall have tribulation: but be of good cheer; I have overcome the world" (John 16:33). Paul exhorted the new converts of south Galatia "to continue in the faith, and that we must through much tribulation enter into the kingdom of God" (Acts 14:22). These tribulations come from the world system because of our identification with Jesus Christ, whom it hated, persecuted, ostracized and crucified. With the apostles, we should rejoice when such trials come because we have been "counted worthy to suffer shame for his name" (Acts 5:41). The Great Tribulation, however, is an altogether different matter. Nowhere in the Scripture are we told that the destiny of the Christian is to enter this period. It is part of the prophetic Day of the Lord, a time of judgment and blessing involving the tribulation, the second advent of Christ, the kingdom rule of Christ, and the destruction of the present universe. The Christian is exempt from this day.

According to Daniel 9:24-27 the tribulation will be a seven-year period, introduced by a covenant made between the Antichrist and Israel. Will this covenant be made immediately after the Church is taken into Heaven? There is some debate here. Some feel that it will start that soon. Others think that there could be an interval between the rapture and the start of the tribulation, an interval up to fifty years. There have been intervals between other dispensations. For example, the age of law ended at the cross, but the Church was not born until Pentecost, fifty days later. If there is an interval (and the Bible is actually silent here), precedent and other Scriptures would seem to argue for a short interval at best. The Scripture, however, is very clear upon the duration of the period; it is seven years long.

The tribulation is also divided into two equal parts of three and one-half years each. There is frequent mention of "time and times and the dividing of time" (Dan. 7:25; Rev. 12:14); forty-two months (Rev. 11:2); and 1,260 days (Rev. 11:3). These two divisions are so marked because the Antichrist breaks off the covenant with Israel in the "midst of the week," or the seven years (Dan. 9:27). The last three and one-half years are terminated by the second coming of Christ to the earth. It may be that the last half of the period will not run its entire course. Jesus said: "Except those days should be shortened, there should no flesh be saved:

but for the elect's sake those days shall be shortened" (Matt. 24:22). Since the exact time of the Lord's coming to the earth is unknown and cannot be determined (Matt. 24:36), He may come before the seven years are up in order to deliver His own from the persecutions of that period.

What will happen in the Great Tribulation? What is its character? First of all, it will be a time of severe divine judgment. God will punish the wicked Gentile nations for their iniquity (Isa. 24:1; 26:21) and for their hatred and mistreatment of God's covenant people, Israel. God promised Abraham, "I will bless them that bless thee, and curse him that curseth thee" (Gen. 12:3). God, always true to His promises, must judge those nations and individuals for their anti-Semitism. The judgments that God will rain down upon the earth will be great and varied—famine, pestilence, earthquakes, lightnings, hail, fire, darkness, insects (Rev. 6:5-8, 16, 17; 8:1-13; 9:1-12). In spite of all of these judgments, men will reveal their sinful dispositions by not turning from their moral and doctrinal error to the living God (Rev. 9:20, 21).

The tribulation is also a time of divine judgment upon Israel. God, through Ezekiel, said many years ago:

> And I will bring you out from the people, and will gather you out of the countries wherein ye are scattered, with a mighty hand, and with a stretched out arm, and with fury poured out.
> And I will bring you into the wilderness of the people, and there will I plead with you face to face.
> And I will cause you to pass under the rod, and I will bring you into the bond of the covenant:
> And I will purge out from among you the rebels, and them that transgress against me . . . (Ezek. 20:34, 35, 37, 38).

After God delivered Israel from Egyptian bondage, they failed to enter Canaan under Moses' leadership because of unbelief. That generation perished in the wilderness. So it will be in the tribulation. Many Jews will be judged because of their lack of faith in Jesus Christ, and for that reason they will die in the tribulation. They will not enter into the blessings of the Millennial Kingdom.

Revelation 16 and 17 describe a strange phenomenon. The apostle John saw a woman riding upon a seven-headed and ten-horned beast. The name of the woman was: "MYSTERY, BABYLON THE GREAT, THE MOTHER OF HARLOTS AND ABOMINATIONS OF THE EARTH" (17:5). This woman represents the last great religious force, the epitome of rebellion against God and self-centeredness. She also has tremendous political and commercial power. Some have identified her as the Roman Catholic Church because she sits on seven mountains or hills. (Tradition states that Rome is built upon seven hills.) It is safer to say that this is apostate Christendom at its worst, composed of all denominations, sects, and isms that profess allegiance to Christ but in reality deny and oppose Him. This religious power is joined to the political empire of the beast, who is the Antichrist. God, who is able to use the actions and attitudes of sinful men to accomplish His ultimate purpose, causes the Antichrist and his satellite leaders to destroy the woman (17:16-18). They do it, but God "remembered her iniquities" (18:5), and "strong is the Lord God who judgeth her" (18:8).

During this period, the Antichrist will not escape the judgment of God. His army and the eastern armies will come together at Armageddon (Rev. 16:12-16), and there Christ will smite them as He treads upon the winepress of the fierceness and wrath of almighty God (Rev. 19:15). This archenemy of God will then be cast into the lake of fire (more on this later).

What about Satan? Even he will experience divine judgment at that time. In the middle of the tribulation period, there will be a war in Heaven between the archangel Michael with God's holy angels and Satan with his unholy angels. Satan will be defeated, and will be cast into the earth. Ever since his sin of pride, Satan has had access into the presence of God (Job 1). He has lived in the heavens. He is certainly the prince of the power of the air and the pinnacle of spiritual wickedness in high places (Eph. 6:12). His heavenly access and activity will be over when he is confined to the earth. This is the beginning of his final judgment. He once said, "I will ascend above the heights of the clouds" (Isa. 14:14). But then he will be cast down into the earth, and later he "shall be brought down to hell, to the sides of the pit" (Isa. 14:15). What a glorious day that will be!

The second key characteristic of the tribulation creates a

paradox. Not only is it a time of severe divine judgment, but it also produces the greatest concentrated revival the world has ever seen. More people, both Jews and Gentiles, will be saved in that seven-year period than in any other equivalent time. For Israel, it will certainly be "Jacob's trouble," but "he shall be saved out of it" (Jer. 30:7). A great number of Israelites in Mount Zion will call upon the Lord for both physical and spiritual deliverance (Joel 2:32). Zechariah indicates that only one-third of the Jews will survive the period as saved people (13:8). God said: "And I will bring the third part through the fire, and will refine them as silver is refined, and will try them as gold is tried: they shall call on my name, and I will hear them: I will say, It is my people, and they shall say, The LORD is my God" (Zech. 13:9). Paul argued that the special spiritual blindness upon the eyes of Israel would be lifted after the "fulness of the Gentiles" had come in (Rom. 11:25). After the Church has been taken into Heaven, "all Israel shall be saved" (Rom. 11:26). Israel will definitely be spiritually prepared for the coming of her Messiah this time, and when she sees Him coming, she will cry out: "Blessed is he that cometh in the name of the Lord" (Matt. 23:39). When they look upon Him whom they pierced and crucified, they shall mourn for Him because of what they had done to Him (Zech. 12:10). The Bible reveals the fact that there will be a special group of Jews (144,000 in number) who will be saved and who will minister during the tribulation. These are twelve thousand out of each of the twelve tribes of Israel (Rev. 7:1-8).

Great hosts of Gentiles will also be saved during the tribulation. John saw and wrote about them: "After this I beheld, and, lo, a great multitude, which no man could number, of all nations, and kindreds, and people, and tongues, stood before the throne, and before the Lamb, clothed with white robes, and palms in their hands" (Rev. 7:9). When he inquired about them, John was told by the angel: "These are they which came out of great tribulation, and have washed their robes, and made them white in the blood of the Lamb" (Rev. 7:14). No one can doubt the clarity of these passages. Thousands and millions of Gentiles throughout the world, not just in one region, will hear the gospel and believe.

This brings us to a logical question. How will they be able to hear the gospel when all of the Christians have been taken into Heaven? "How then shall they call on him in whom they have not believed? and how shall they believe in him of whom they have not heard? and how shall they hear without a preacher" (Rom. 10:14)? Faith comes only by hearing the preached word of God, but where are the preachers? First of all, God will providentially raise up two witnesses to preach for three and one-half years (Rev. 11:3-12). Perhaps Christ will manifest Himself to them even as He did to Paul on the Damascus road (Acts 9), a revelation from Heaven. These two will have a ministry similar to that of Moses and Elijah. They will cause it not to rain, will turn water into blood, and will bring plagues upon the earth. After they are martyred, they will be resurrected and will ascend into Heaven. Such a demonstration of divine power will bring fear and wonder to the people (perhaps even belief).

The 144,000 Jews, called "the servants of our God" (Rev. 7:3), could have a universal ministry at this time. The Jews are excellent missionary prospects. They live throughout the world, and they read and speak many languages. When the Jerusalem church was persecuted, the Jewish believers were scattered abroad and went everywhere preaching the Word (Acts 8:4). Once these 144,000 Jews are regenerated, they will be persecuted. Their natural flight will take them into the remote corners of the earth where they will share their faith with others.

In addition to these human means, it appears that God will also use an angel (maybe more than one):

> And I saw another angel fly in the midst of heaven, having the everlasting gospel to preach unto them that dwell on the earth, and to every nation, and kindred, and tongue, and people,
> Saying with a loud voice, Fear God, and give glory to him; for the hour of his judgment is come: and worship him that made heaven, and earth, and the sea, and the fountains of waters (Rev. 14:6, 7).

Just as God used angels to warn Lot to flee from the coming judgment of Sodom, so He will use an angel to warn the world against the judgment to come. Through both natural and supernatural means, all of the world will have an opportunity to hear the gospel.

Now, what is this gospel which will be preached? Will it be the same as that voiced behind evangelical pulpits today? The angel will cry out: "Fear God, give glory to Him, and worship Him." Jesus said: "And this gospel of the kingdom shall be preached in all the world for a witness unto all nations; and then shall the end come" (Matt. 24:14). The gospel of the kingdom is the same message that John the Baptist, Jesus, and His disciples preached 2000 years ago: "Repent ye: for the kingdom of heaven is at hand" (Matt. 3:2; 4:17; 10:7). Spiritual repentance and conversion are necessary for entrance into the kingdom of God which will be established upon the earth when Jesus returns. In the tribulation, they will preach that the Kingdom promised in the Old Testament, offered in the gospel era, postponed during the Church Age, will soon be established by the return of Jesus Christ to the earth. They will declare that He was the one who was crucified for their sins, buried, and who was raised from the dead. The nearness of His coming, supported by the judgments of God, will produce an urgency both to preach and to believe.

How can ministers preach and how can people believe if the Holy Spirit is not in the world then? No one can preach in the power of his own strength (Acts 1:8), and no one can be saved apart from the convicting, regenerating work of the Holy Spirit (John 3:5; 16:7-11). Many have the idea that when the Church is raptured, the Holy Spirit, Who indwells believers, will also be taken into Heaven and that He will be absent from the earth. This is a misconception based upon this Pauline passage: "For the mystery of iniquity doth already work: only he who now letteth will let, until he be taken out of the way" (2 Thess. 2:7). This verse deals with the Spirit's work of restraining open sin in the world, not with His presence. It must be remembered that the Spirit of God was in the world before He descended in a unique way on the Day of Pentecost to form the Church. He is God, and as God, He is omnipresent. He is everywhere present at all times in the totality of His being. When the Church is taken into Heaven, He will end His work of baptism (1 Cor. 12:13), but He will still be in the world. The retarding effect of the Church (salt of the earth, light of the world) will, of course, be gone. Even the Spirit will not restrain sin then as He does today. He will permit sin and sinners to have their day. Nothing will hold back the expression of open sin in that time. The always present Spirit of God, therefore, will have a definite ministry in the tribulation.

Invariably, the next question is always asked about the tribulation. Will people have a second chance to hear and to believe? If a person rejects Christ during this Church Age, will he be able to believe after the Church has been raptured? The first problem to solve is a definition of second chance. If you mean by it only one opportunity to hear, then all people get a second chance—yes, even a third, fourth, etc. How many people accept Jesus Christ as personal Savior the very first time they hear about Him? Very seldom does that happen. God manifested His long-suffering grace to all of us by continuing to work with our stubborn wills. Usually, though, second chance refers to a second opportunity in the tribulation. Most preachers have argued that the only people who will be saved in the tribulation will be those who have never heard the name of Christ during this Church Age. There is only one passage of Scripture that seems to touch on this subject:

> And with all deceivableness of unrighteousness in them that perish; because they received not the love of the truth, that they might be saved.
> And for this cause God shall send them strong delusion, that they should believe a lie:
> That they all might be damned who believed not the truth, but had pleasure in unrighteousness (2 Thess. 2:10-12).

Those who received not, believed not and lived for pleasure *in this age* will be so deceived in the tribulation that they will accept *the* lie. They will accept a man, the Antichrist, as God. This is a plausible explanation of the passage; however, it does not clearly state the *time* of the original rejection. It may be that those who reject the gospel *in the first half of the tribulation* will then accept the delusion of the Antichrist. Since so many Jews will be saved, it is hard to imagine that none of those ever heard of the Christian message in the Church Age. Certainly, in our appeal to the unsaved, we should not encourage them to put off a decision for Christ. They should not procrastinate. They should not boast themselves of tomorrow, for who knows what tomorrow will bring? "Now is the accepted time; behold, now is the day of salvation" (2 Cor. 6:2). It definitely will not be easier to accept Christ in the tribulation than it is today. In that day, receiving

Christ will bring severe persecution and possible martyrdom; it is not so today.

The mention of persecution brings us to the third major characteristic of the Great Tribulation. It will not only be a time of divine judgment, an era of human salvation, but also, an unprecedented period of severe persecution. Jesus warned the persecuted ones of that day with these words:

> Then let them which be in Judaea flee into the mountains:
> Let him which is on the housetop not come down to take any thing out of his house:
> Neither let him which is in the field return back to take his clothes.
> And woe unto them that are with child, and to them that give suck in those days!
> But pray ye that your flight be not in the winter, neither on the sabbath day:
> For then shall be great tribulation, such as was not since the beginning of the world to this time, no, nor ever shall be (Matt. 24:16-21).

What prompts this quick escape is the coming of the Antichrist and his subsequent persecution of the nation of Israel. Jesus called him the abomination of desolation (Matt. 24:15) because he would ravage the Jews. Daniel said that he would wear out the (Jewish) "saints of the most High" (Dan. 7:25). The Antichrist will also persecute Gentiles who have been kind to the fleeing Jews, who have accepted the gospel message, and who have refused to worship him. All who do not worship an image or idol of this deceiver will be killed (Rev. 13:15). When John saw the saints in Heaven, he heard them cry: "How long, O Lord, holy and true, dost thou not judge and avenge our blood on them that dwell on the earth" (Rev. 6:10)? They were told that more of their fellow servants and brethren would be killed even as they were (Rev. 6:11). The Antichrist will hate, persecute and kill all those who dare to be identified with Jesus Christ. The Antichrist will also slay the two witnesses that God will introduce. He will display their bodies for three and one-half days in the streets of Jerusalem (Rev. 11:3-12).

The persecution of Israel by the Antichrist is caused by Satan's hatred of Israel, the nation which produced Jesus Christ. After Satan is cast into the earth by Michael in the middle of the tribulation period, he will pour out his spite toward God upon Israel. When he will be cast out, the dwellers of Heaven can rejoice, but John warned the earth: "Woe to the inhabitants of the earth and of the sea! for the devil is come down unto you, having great wrath, because he knoweth that he hath but a short time" (Rev. 12:12). When Satan begins to persecute Israel, God will miraculously preserve her in the wilderness. Some have said that Israel will find refuge in the ancient region of Edom, where Petra is located. It may be that at this time God will reinstitute the miracle of manna. Just as God daily fed the nation during the wilderness wanderings, so He will supply nourishment for persecuted Israel. Since no one can buy or sell unless they have the mark of the beast (Rev. 13:17), the manna will come in response to their prayer: "Thy kingdom come. Thy will be done in earth, as it is in heaven. Give us this day our daily bread" (Matt. 6:10, 11). Since he can't destroy the nation, he will "make war with the remnant of her seed, which keep the commandments of God, and have the testimony of Jesus Christ" (Rev. 12:17).

The child of God can thank the Lord for the fact that he will not be exposed to the persecutions of this dreadful period. Our blessed Savior will come and take us into Heaven before the Great Tribulation begins. Only unsaved people will go into that era in their natural bodies. During that time, many will be saved, persecuted and martyred. When the tribulation ends, only the saved, both Jews and Gentiles, who have endured the persecutions, will be permitted to enter the Millennial Kingdom. All of the living unsaved will be cast into everlasting punishment at that time. Thus will end the darkest era of human history.

6 – WHAT ARE THE SIGNS
OF HIS COMING?

IN THE FULLNESS of time, God sent forth His Son (Gal. 4:4). He was born in the right place (Bethlehem), at the right time (Roman supremacy), and in the right way (virgin born). That coming, promised in the Old Testament, was announced by signs. The sudden appearance of a new star convinced the Magi that the King of the Jews had been born (Matt. 2:2). When the Pharisees and Sadducees asked Jesus for a sign from Heaven, He criticized them: "O ye hypocrites, ye can discern the face of the sky; but can ye not discern the signs of the times?" (Matt. 16:3). They were able to predict the weather by observing the sky; they should have known from the Scriptures and from observation of Him that prophecy was being fulfilled before their very eyes. Later, at the triumphal entry, Jesus wept over the city of Jerusalm because its inhabitants did not know "in this thy day, the things which belong unto thy peace" and "the time of thy visitation" (Luke 19:42, 44). Concentrated interest in just plain, everyday activities had made dull their spiritual sensitivity. They should have known that the Messiah was to come in their generation, but they did not.

As a result of His rejection by Israel, Jesus began to prepare His disciples for His coming death and resurrection and for His absence from the earth. After His lamentation over Jerusalem, He said to the city (representing the nation): "Ye shall not see me henceforth, till ye shall say, Blessed is he that cometh in the name of the Lord" (Matt. 23:39). Here Jesus predicted a time of absence, a return, and a joyful reception by Israel at His second advent. Later, on the Mount of Olives, the disciples asked him privately, "Tell us, when shall these things be? and what shall be the sign of thy coming, and of the end of the world?" (Matt. 24:3). In His reply, called the Olivet Discourse (Matt. 24, 25; Mark 13; Luke 21), Jesus outlined the events that would have to take place before He would return to the earth. These signs (or events) are *not* signs of the rapture of the Church, but signs of His coming to the earth which will be visible and which will be accepted by Israel. This coming takes place after the Great Tribulation:

> Immediately after the tribulation of those days shall the sun be darkened, and the moon shall not give her light, and the stars shall fall from heaven, and the powers of the heavens shall be shaken:
> And then shall appear the sign of the Son of man in heaven: and then shall all the tribes of the earth mourn, and they shall see the Son of man coming in the clouds of heaven with power and great glory (Matt. 24:29, 30).

These signs, then, will have their complete fulfillment in the Great Tribulation. However, since just seven years may separate the rapture from His return to the earth, it is very logical to conclude that the embryonic beginnings of the signs could be seen in the end of the Church Age. What we see today taking place in the world should not be regarded as *the* signs of His coming, only as feelers, giving us the direction of the wind. We are certainly closer to the coming of the Lord today than the disciples were. Our heartbeat and pulse should quicken a little as we view current events in the light of Scripture. We may be living in the last days of the Church Age. Just as shadows indicate the presence of the sun, so the shadows of the signs indicate the Parousia of the Son. The signs of the tribulation do, in fact, cast their shadows back into the Church Age.

The first sign that Jesus mentioned was the appearance of *false messiahs.* He said: "Take heed that no man deceive you. For many shall come in my name, saying, I am Christ; and shall deceive many" (Matt. 24:4, 5). There will be *many* false Christs (self-appointed, self-anointed ones) before the revelation of the *one* personal Antichrist, the one who opposes Jesus Christ and who offers himself as a substitute for the real Savior. The world has always welcomed saviors who promised deliverance from racial, economic, religious, social and national ills. It has marched, picketed, demonstrated, fought, died and given for new causes led by dynamic, charismatic personalities. In New Testament times, an insurrection against the Roman government was led by Barabbas. Our Lord's popularity with the masses to some extent was due to His denunciation of the status quo and the offer of a new type of life. Even Paul was mistaken for an Egyptian insurrectionist leader of four thousand murderers (Acts 21:38).

Down through the centuries, new political movements have been created and led by gifted individuals: Marxism with Lenin and Stalin; Nazism with Hitler; Fascism with Mussolini. Religious cults and isms have centered on their founders. In our own day, we have black nationalism among the emerging African nations; black power here in the States; Castroism; and Red Chinese communism. When political leaders go on a campaign, there is mob, Hollywood-idol, hysteria present. It doesn't take much imagination to conceive of a day when a bright, handsome, magnetic leader would be followed, even worshiped, if he would offer the world a universal solution for the ills and injustices of mankind—for the racial problems, for poverty, for juvenile delinquency, for the big city, ghetto problems, for student rebellions, and for the easing of East-West tension. These false messiahs will increase in number and deception as we approach the end of the age and enter into the Great Tribulation. It would appear that some of them will try to pass themselves off as the real Jesus Christ, returned from Heaven:

> Then if any man shall say unto you, Lo, here is Christ, or there; believe it not.
> For there shall arise false Christs, and false prophets, and shall shew great signs and wonders; insomuch that, if it were possible, they shall deceive the very elect.
> Behold, I have told you before.
> Wherefore, if they shall say unto you, Behold, he is in the desert; go not forth: behold, he is in the secret chambers; believe it not (Matt. 24:23-26).

The deception will be so clever that it will almost fool God's own people. Just as Christ's first coming was announced by John the Baptist and His second will be by the two witnesses (Rev. 11), so these false Christs are introduced by false prophets. Just as Jesus supported His claims with divine miracles, so these false messiahs will perform supernatural signs in the power of Satan or magic. The person who has heard and rejected the gospel message over and over in this age will be a ripe candidate for such deception after the Church has been taken into Heaven. Such a person will be convinced of the truth of the Bible when he sees that his Christian friends have vanished as they mentioned in their witness to Him. Then this false messiah will appear and claim that he sent the Christians on into Heaven and that he had returned to the earth as he had said before. This person will not be able to distinguish the truth and the error of these claims, and so, he will fall for the delusion. Jesus said to watch out for false Christs.

Jesus then spoke of *national and international unrest:* "And ye shall hear of wars and rumours of wars: see that ye be not troubled: for all these things must come to pass, but the end is not yet. For nation shall rise against nation, and kingdom against kingdom" (Matt. 24:6, 7a). The history of mankind has been the history of war. There always has been war, and there always will be war. Peace is not around the corner or at the next negotiation table. There will not be any international peace until the Prince of Peace returns to the earth and rules over a kingdom of righteousness and peace with a rod of iron. Wars and rumors of wars, both in quantity and severity, will increase as we move closer to the tribulation era. In the short history of the United States, there has been the Revolutionary War, the War of 1812, the Civil War, the Spanish-American War, World War I, World War II, the Korean conflict and Vietnam (besides some lesser campaigns). In eighty years of this century, our country has matched the four previous major wars. Look at the world situation today. The nations are sitting on a thermonuclear bomb and the fuse is about to be lit. All it would take would be one slight misunderstanding, one miscalculation or one frenzied act by a madman. Do we really have a fail-safe system? Look at the tensions: Vietnam, Cuba, Arab-Israel, Red China-India, Red China-Russia, Russia-her satellites, Russia-United States, Cyprus and NATO-France. These political and ideological pressures, tensions and differences will continue even until Jesus Christ comes. Don't put your confidence in the United Nations or in Geneva conferences; place it in Him.

Jesus then mentioned that "there shall be famines, and pestilences, and earthquakes, in divers places" (Matt. 24:7b). These *natural disasters* have often occurred in the past, but Jesus indicated that there would be a sharp increase in these strange phenomena as His coming to the earth drew near. It is a paradox that in the richest country of the world with tremendous natural resources and means of mass production there are great pockets of poverty and physical deprivation. Some have conjectured that over half of the world's population goes to bed hungry. Under-developed countries just can't produce food fast enough for the population explosion. There have been great crop failures in many countries, especially in Red China, in recent years. In the Book of Revelation, three of the first six seal judgments that God will pour out on the earth can be equated with these natural signs (Rev. 6:5-8, 12-17). The third horse of the Apocalypse represented famine. It was black, and John "heard a voice in the midst of the four beasts say, A measure of wheat for a penny, and three measures of barley for a penny; and see thou hurt not the oil and the wine" (Rev. 6:6). The fourth horse, ridden by Death and Hell, had power "over the fourth part of the earth, to kill with sword [wars], and with hunger [famine], and with death [pestilence], and with the beasts of the earth" (Rev. 6:8).

After Jesus mentioned these first three sign areas, He stated: "All these are the beginning of sorrows. Then shall they deliver you up to be afflicted" (Matt. 24:8, 9a). Since the Antichrist will not break his covenant with Israel until the middle of the tribulation (Dan. 9:27) with subsequent persecution of the Jews as a result, it would appear that these first signs mentioned (false Christs, wars, natural phenomena) will take place in the first half of the tribulation.

Not only will strange things occur on earth, but there will also be *signs in the heavens:* ". . . fearful sights and great signs shall there be from heaven" (Luke 21:11). Some have thought that flying saucers and other unidentified flying objects (UFO's) which have been reported with unusual repetition in recent years could be the fulfillment of this prophecy. However, the signs that Jesus mentioned were to be witnessed by the world at large, not by just a few individuals. He said:

> And there shall be signs in the sun, and in the moon, and in the stars; and upon the earth distress of nations, with perplexity; the sea and the waves roaring;
> Men's hearts failing them for fear, and for looking after those things which are coming on the earth: for the powers of heaven shall be shaken (Luke 21:25, 26).

Something unusual is going to happen in the sky. The moon's control of the ocean tides will be changed, causing huge tidal waves. John said that the sun will become black as sackcloth of hair, that the moon will be as blood (red in color), that the stars will fall, and that the heaven will be rolled together as a scroll (Rev. 6:12-14). All of the world will see these signs and will be affected by them. These signs are not being seen today, but they will be manifested during the tribulation, probably in the middle and latter years of that era. Astronomers will be puzzled by the heavenly distortions; there will be no logical, naturalistic explanation for the phenomena. Laymen will be afraid, and sinners will hide themselves in caves, crying out to the mountains and rocks: "Fall on us, and hide us from the face of him that sitteth on the throne, and from the wrath of the Lamb: For the great day of his wrath is come; and who shall be able to stand" (Rev. 6:16, 17)? Whoever heard of the wrath *of a lamb,* but here it is! The day of the vindication of our God will strike fear into the hearts of unbelieving men.

Jesus said that the conditions on earth prior to His coming would be like those in the time of Noah: "For as in the days that were before the flood they were eating and drinking, marrying and giving in marriage, until the day that Noe entered into the ark, And knew not until the flood came, and took them all away; so shall also the coming of the Son of man be" (Matt. 24:38, 39). At first glance, it would seem that gross wickedness and iniquity would be present on the earth then. Gluttony, drunkenness, common-law marriage and divorce would be normal experiences then. It is true that Noah's era was extremely sinful. The flood judgment came because "God saw that the wickedness of man was great in the earth, and that every imagination of the thoughts of his heart was only evil continually" (Gen. 6:5).

But was Jesus simply referring to terrible sins? He also equated the latter times with the days of Lot: "They did eat, they drank, they bought, they sold, they planted, they builded" (Luke 17:28). There is nothing sinful in eating, drinking, buying, selling, planting and building. These are normal, everyday activities. Why then did Jesus mention these things? It was because *secularism* and *materialism* would make men *indifferent* and *insensitive* to the warnings of imminent divine judgment. This is the condition that will mark the tribulation period. The people in Noah's time ignored Noah's warning; they went about daily pursuits with indifference toward his construction of an ark. They lived for today and planned for the future without any regard that God would or could judge them. And this is what we can see today. The world is concerned about cars, college, cottages and crabgrass, not about conversion. On any given Sunday morning, a family can rise, eat breakfast, read the paper, hitch the boat trailer to the car, drive by ten evangelical churches with "Jesus Saves" signs in front of them, spend a day at the beach, drive past those same churches again at night, retire for the night, and not have a bothered conscience! People live today as though they are going to live forever. The comfortable, affluent, high standard of living in our country has been used by Satan to lull people into spiritual insensitivity. They are living for things and today; they just do not care about Christ and eternity. This attitude, increased in intensity, will be a characteristic of the end time.

In his last letter, Paul described the condition of *moral laxity and apostasy* that would characterize the last days of the Church Age. Since Christ's return to the earth is only about seven years after the end of the Church Age, this sign is also indicative of the end time:

> This know also, that in the last days perilous times shall come.
>
> For men shall be lovers of their own selves, covetous, boasters, proud, blasphemers, disobedient to parents, unthankful, unholy,
>
> Without natural affection, trucebreakers, false accusers, incontinent, fierce, despisers of those that are good,
>
> Traitors, heady, highminded, lovers of pleasures more than lovers of God;
>
> Having a form of godliness, but denying the power thereof: from such turn away (2 Tim. 3:1-5).

Compare this prophecy with the front pages of our nation's newspapers! Is not this a description of our day? Today men will not get involved in the affairs of others because they are so self-centered. They can watch an old man get beaten by a bunch of thugs, pull the shade, sit down, and watch television. As Cain, they are not their brother's keeper. Juvenile delinquency is just the by-product of parental delinquency. Disobedience toward civil authorities is the result of saying no to Dad and getting away with it. Look at how unthankful welfare recipients are. They march and picket for greater benefits. Many believe that the world automatically owes them a living because of their deprived state. There was a time when families had so much self-respect that they would refuse handouts. Homosexuality has crawled out of the gutter and now has an air of respectability around it. Contracts and negotiated agreements are no longer binding, even with affixed signatures. You can't shake on it anymore! A man's word means nothing today, sad to say. Our nation has been rocked by violence and crime in our metropolitan areas. It is not safe to walk the streets. Even policemen are afraid to patrol by themselves. The savage characteristics of the children in *Lord of the Flies* can be seen in the teenage gangs with their zip guns and switchblade knives. Attitudes toward good, moral people have radically changed. Today such a person is square, out of it, no earthly good, or holier than thou. Carnivals, auto races, sunbathing, love-ins and pot are more relevant than God. And yet church attendance is up. Why? There is a *form* of godliness, but there is no power. There are no inner dynamics; there is no indwelling Holy Spirit. The form is good for business and respectability; but they are too self-sufficient to admit their need of Christ.

Not only moral defection, but *doctrinal apostasy* will also mark the last days. Paul wrote: "Now the Spirit speaketh expressly, that in the latter times some shall depart from the faith, giving heed to seducing spirits, and doctrines of devils" (1 Tim. 4:1). Denials of God and of the Bible are becoming more vocal in our time. What was once whispered behind seminary library doors is now being preached on the housetops. *God is dead!* What a declaration that is! We could expect it from an atheist outside the church, but the advocates of this Christian atheism are ordained ministers, with doctorates in theology, teaching and preaching in church-related institutions. Someone once wrote a book entitled *How To Become a Bishop Without Being Religious.* What a true observation! Can you imagine an Episcopal bishop trying to contact the spirit of his dead son through a spiritualist medium! And yet that happened. The new immorality, or situation ethics as it is commonly called, has been pushed by clergymen. Is this not "seducing spirits and doctrines of devils"? The historic Westminster Confession of Faith has now been altered to allow for belief in a non-inspired, errant

Bible. Most laymen are unaware of the gross attacks that are made upon the integrity of the Bible by professors of religion. Moses did not write the Pentateuch; Daniel did not write Daniel; Ruth, Jonah and Esther are fictional short stories; the gospel biographies misrepresented the Person and ministry of Christ in their writings—these are just a few examples.

Paul also mentioned that "the time will come when they will not endure sound doctrine; but after their own lusts shall they heap to themselves teachers, having itching ears; And they shall turn away their ears from the truth, and shall be turned unto fables" (2 Tim. 4:3, 4). In modern church services, there is often a preference for jazz over Jesus, for dancing over doctrine, and for church suppers over salvation. The twentieth century has become the era of innovation for the church, and it can be seen in the rise and fall of doctrinal heresies (liberalism, neoorthodoxy, neoliberalism, demythologization) at the expense of abandoning the true faith of the Scriptures.

The Book of Revelation indicates that the *organized church of the latter times* will be materially rich and self-sufficient, but spiritually poor and needy (Rev. 3:14-19). The story is told of a visitor to the Vatican who praised the wealth of the church to a papal representative. The latter replied, "Peter said, 'Silver and gold have I none' (Acts 3:6). But the church cannot say that now." The visitor then reacted, "Yes, that is true, but neither can you say, '. . . rise up and walk' " (Acts 3:6). The church has lost in gaining. This Laodicean type church will develop into the ecumenical, one-world church of the Great Tribulation and will join itself unknowingly to the political power of the Antichrist (Rev. 17, 18). In that day, the organized, apostate church will bear the infamous title: "MYSTERY, BABYLON THE GREAT, THE MOTHER OF HARLOTS AND ABOMINATIONS OF THE EARTH" (Rev. 17:5). It will be opposed to true evangelicals and will in fact cause their martyrdom. "Babylon" is a significant title. It was at Babel that men tried to gain the presence of God through human effort based upon human pride (Gen. 11). The future church will be just that—man centered, not God centered and motivated.

The future ecumenical church will be composed of all sects within professing Christendom that deny the necessity of Christ's death and resurrection as the means into God's presence. The current climate of church mergers and ecumenical councils is reversing the spirit of the Reformation. Liberal Protestants are getting together and joining with Roman Catholics for the first time in over 450 years. Newspapers have reported that Protestants and Catholics have now agreed upon a common reading of the Lord's Prayer and of the Apostles' Creed. In fact, these groups are moving toward a common Bible. Five years of translation work have culminated in an eight-page document entitled "Guiding Principles of Interconfessional Cooperation in Translating the Bible." This union is based upon political and organizational lines, not upon doctrinal and moral oneness. There is union, but not unity.

Daniel was told that in the time of the end *knowledge would be increased* (Dan. 12:4). Today we are in such a knowledge explosion. Educational researchers have reported that our knowledge is doubling every ten years. Imagine that! Take all of the knowledge learned from the creation of Adam to the present and we will learn its equivalent in the next ten years. Scientific and medical technology is running far ahead of the human mind. This is why the science of cybernetics was invented—to give us computers to store this vast area of facts for future usage. Libraries and universities are going to microfilm and computer consoles. The general practitioner (of anything) is on his way out. Today one must specialize. He must know a lot about a little. In our own century, we have gone from the horse and buggy to the space capsule, from grass to Astroturf, and from walking to the monorail. And it wasn't until this century that the world had seen such advances. Expect more, for knowledge will continue to increase until Jesus comes.

The Bible also reveals the fact that during the great tribulation period there will be *four major military powers* in the world. The nation of Israel will be in control of Palestine (to be discussed in the next chapter), surrounded by these four powers—eastern, western, southern and northern. The western power will be the revived Roman Empire, led by the Antichrist (Dan. 9:26). The land area covered by the old Roman Empire can now be seen in the western European nations or the NATO alliance. The power of the north (Ezek. 38, 39) can be equated with Soviet Russia. Even before the Communist or Bolshevik Revolution in 1917, Bible commentators had identified the fulfillment of this prophecy with Russia. The Southern Kingdom (Dan. 11:5) can be identified with the Pan-Arab alliance, led by Egypt, or with the Black African countries (or possibly with both). The kings of the east (Rev. 16:12) can be seen in Red China with her satellite oriental neighbors. Never in the history of the world have these four major powers been in existence at the same time. In addition, Israel is now back in the land for the first time in nineteen hundred years. If God ever wanted to introduce the Great Tribulation, He couldn't ask for a better time than this. The stage is set; the players (nations) are prepared; all it needs is God's predetermined time and a human error. Then the nations will begin to move rapidly toward the hub of the earth (see chapter on Armageddon).

Jesus said that when we are able to perceive these signs, then we would be able to know that the kingdom of God was near. His coming to the earth would take place during the generation of those who actually began to see the signs (Luke 21:31, 32). If the signs mentioned above are really having their beginnings today, then we are definitely in the last days. As Paul said: "Now is our salvation nearer than when we believed" (Rom. 13:11). Because of this, it is high time to awake out of our spiritual insensitivity. "The night is far spent, the day is at hand: let us therefore cast off the works of darkness, and let us put on the armour of light" (Rom. 13:12). Remember that these are signs of His second coming to the earth after the tribulation. There are no signs for the pretribulational rapture of the Church. But indications of the nearness of His second advent make the rapture appear that much closer.

> Signs of His coming multiply,
> Morning light breaks in eastern sky;
> Watch, for the time is drawing nigh—
> What if it were today?

7 – WHAT ABOUT ISRAEL?

ISRAEL IS THE MOST remarkable nation upon the face of the globe. Ancient nations have appeared and vanished (Assyria, Babylon, etc.), but Israel stands. Emigrant peoples have been absorbed by the countries into which they went, but not so with the Jews. They have remained a distinctive people, both racially and religiously, throughout the centuries. Fear, flight, persecution, martyrdom—these have not altered the Jewish image. As ever, so now, Israel stands indeed as God's chosen people. Just before his death, Moses reminded the Israelites of their divine heritage and national distinctiveness:

> For thou art an holy people unto the LORD thy God: the LORD thy God hath chosen thee to be a special people unto himself, above all people that are upon the face of the earth.
>
> The LORD did not set his love upon you, nor choose you, because ye were more in number than any people; for ye were the fewest of all people:
>
> But because the LORD loved you, and because he would keep the oath which he had sworn unto your fathers, hath the LORD brought you out with a mighty hand, and redeemed you out of the house of bondmen, from the hand of Pharaoh king of Egypt (Deut. 7:6-8).

God purposed that Israel would be a holy, chosen, special and free nation. It was not His design that Israel would have the largest population or military might among the countries of the world, but that Israel would be a pure testimony to the oneness and holiness of God (Deut. 6:4). God's sovereign choice was not based upon anything special within the Jewish people, but simply upon the fact that God willed to set His love upon Israel for His greater glory.

The history of Israel began with the call of God to Abraham, the father of the Hebrew nation, to leave Ur of the Chaldees and to go to the Promised Land (Canaan or Palestine). The early history of the Hebrews is centered in the lives of the patriarchs—Abraham, Isaac, Jacob (or Israel) and his twelve sons, especially Joseph. The names of the twelve sons later became the titles of the twelve tribes of Israel. At the request of Joseph, the small Jewish family (about seventy), including Jacob, went down into Egypt. There the family multiplied into a nation so that four hundred years later they numbered about two to three million strong. However, the people were then in slave bondage to the Egyptians.

Through the intervention of ten divine plagues and the human leadership of Moses, the people of Israel came out of Egypt, crossed the divinely opened Red Sea, and marched on to Mount Sinai. At Sinai God gave to Moses the Ten Commandments plus the other moral, civil and ceremonial regulations. At this site they also constructed the Tabernacle, the portable worship center, according to God's specifications. From Sinai they traveled to Kadesh-Barnea, on the southern threshhold of the Promised Land. Here the nation stubbornly refused to enter because of their fear of the Canaanites and their lack of faith in God. God then punished them by causing them to wander in the wilderness for the next forty years. They finally came to the plains of Moab, on the eastern side of the Jordan River, where Moses died and Joshua took over.

Under Joshua's leadership, the people crossed the supernaturally parted, flooding Jordan River, invaded the land, and conquered the various confederations of Canaanite city-kingdoms. The land was distributed among the twelve tribes with each family receiving an allotted portion.

After the death of Joshua, the nation sank into its darkest era, the period of the judges, when everyone did that which was right in his own eyes. Personal, religious and national anarchy and apostasy were everywhere. God again chastised them by causing the surrounding nations to oppress them. When the people cried out in repentance, God raised up judges to deliver them and to guide them during a time of peace. At the death of the judge, the nation would again slip into its sinful disobedience. Tiring of direct theocratic leadership and the uncertain "judge—no judge" atmosphere, the nation desired a king so intensely that Samuel, the last judge, anointed Saul to become the first king.

The kingdom era had started. Saul was followed by David, then Solomon. During the reigns of the latter two, Israel was the strongest and most prosperous nation in the Near Eastern world. During Solomon's reign, the famous Temple was built. The Jewish kingdom divided after the death of Solomon into two sections—the Northern Kingdom of ten tribes or Israel and the Southern Kingdom of two tribes or Judah. These two kingdoms existed side by side for about two centuries (931-722 B.C.) with strong hostility usually between them. Finally Israel was conquered by Assyria with her leading citizens dispersed throughout the pagan empire. Judah withstood the onslaught, persevered for another century, but was finally destroyed by Babylon. The Gentile power laid waste the city of Jerusalem, breaking down both the city walls and Solomon's Temple. The leading citizens of the Southern Kingdom were taken as captives into Babylon. After seventy years of captivity, the Jews were permitted by the new world power, the Medo-Persians, to return to Palestine to build a new temple. Under the leadership of Zerubbabel, Haggai and Zechariah, this was accomplished. Later waves of Jewish refugees followed, full of love for their homeland, accompanied by a desire to repopulate Jerusalem and to rebuild her walls. At the end of Old Testament history, the Jews were again back in Palestine under Persian control worshiping God at the new temple.

For the next four hundred years, the Jews remained in the Promised Land as tenants with the landlords changing from time to time—first the Persians, then the Greeks, followed by the Egyptian Ptolemies, the Syrian Seleucidae, a brief period of Maccabean-Hasmonean freedom, and finally the iron clutches of the Roman Empire were around them. For some six hundred years, the people rested in the prophetic hope that one day the divine-human Messiah would come, destroy the pagan forces, and establish a kingdom of peace, prosperity and righteousness.

The Messiah, in the Person of Jesus Christ, did arrive, but the nation in its spiritual blindness and sin rejected the offer of the King. Instead the leaders put Him on the cross. For this sin God caused the Romans to destroy the city of Jerusalem, blasting the walls, leveling Herod's remodeled Temple, and scattering the people. From that time (A.D. 70) to our present generation, the Jews have been a people without a country. In our own day, we have seen prophecy being fulfilled before our very eyes. Some have called it a miracle. Israel now has a land, and the Star of David again flies over ancient Jerusalem. This brief history should help you understand the Biblical significance of present happenings and the prospects of the future.

Israel alone is God's privileged, covenant nation. Paul described her divine blessings in this way: "Who are Israelites; to whom pertaineth the adoption, and the glory, and the covenants, and the giving of the law, and the service of God, and the promises" (Rom. 9:4). The entire basis of the relationship that exists between God and Israel is the unconditional character of the four covenants that God made with her. The fulfillment of these covenants does not rest upon the obedience or faithfulness of the Jews; it rests solely upon the faithfulness of God to His Word. He cannot lie, and He will do what He has promised. The first covenant, the Abrahamic (Gen. 12:1-3; 13:14-18; 15:1-21; 17:1-8), guaranteed that out of Abraham would come a great nation (Israel); that Abraham would become wealthy; that his name would be revered (it is by Christian, Jew and Muslim); that love of the Jew would be rewarded; that anti-Semitism would be punished; that the entire world would be spiritually blessed by the seed of Abraham, who is Christ; that the entire land of Palestine from Egypt to Assyria would be the permanent possession of the Jews; that several nations would come out of His loins (Israel, Arab peoples, Midian, etc.); and that he would be a father of kings. This covenant was reiterated to Isaac and to Jacob. God was to be known as the God of Abraham, Isaac and Jacob.

At the end of his career, Moses anticipated the time when the Jews would commit spiritual adultery and God would consequently drive them out of the Promised Land. However, this dispersion was to be only temporary. In the Palestinian Covenant (Deut. 29, 30), Moses also foresaw the time in which the people would repent and turn again unto God. God would respond by bringing them out of captivity into the land; by giving them personal and national salvation from both their sins and their oppressors; by judging their enemies; and by prospering them in their economic pursuits in the land. No doubt these words encouraged the invading Jewish army under Joshua's guidance, and they should equally comfort the Jew of today as he returns to his fatherland.

The Davidic Covenant (2 Sam. 7:11-16) focused on the kingdom promises. David was told that Solomon, his son, would rule after him; that Solomon would build the temple; that Solomon would not be treated for his sins as Saul was; and that his *house, throne* and *kingdom* would be established *forever*. Those last three words are the important ones. When the angel Gabriel came to Mary to announce God's purpose, he predicted:

> And, behold, thou shalt conceive in thy womb, and bring forth a son, and shalt call his name JESUS.
> He shall be great, and shall be called the Son of the Highest: and the Lord God shall give unto him the throne of his father David:
> And he shall reign over the house of Jacob for ever; and of his kingdom there shall be no end (Luke 1:31-33).

The promises given to David were to be ultimately and completely fulfilled in the Person and work of Jesus Christ. Christ has not yet established this kingdom; He has not yet ruled over Israel; He has not ascended to David's throne yet. The greater fulfillment of this covenant is still future.

The final covenant was given shortly before Judah fell to the Babylonians. However, it was made with *all* of the twelve tribes even though ten of them (the Northern Kingdom) had been scattered over a century before. It was called the New Covenant because it was to supplant the old, conditional, Mosaic Covenant made at Sinai. Instead of being written upon tables of stone, it was to be carved upon the tissues of the Jewish hearts. God promised that He would always be their God; that they would always be His people; that one day every Jew would know Him in sincerity and truth; and that their sins and iniquities would forever be erased. The night before He was crucified, our Lord instituted the communion meal at which He said concerning the wine, "This is the blood of the new covenant." When He shed His blood upon that cruel cross, He not only was bearing the penalty of the sins of the entire world, but He was also establishing the foundation for the final fulfillment of the New Covenant with Israel. It might be added that all of the covenants made with Israel had their origin in God's grace and that the support of His giving grace is centered in the cross of Calvary. It is a paradox, but when Israel put to death Jesus Christ, she was actually making possible the fulfillment of her covenants. As Paul said: "O the depth of the riches both of the wisdom and knowledge of God! how unsearchable are his judgments, and his ways past finding out" (Rom. 11:33)!

As God's covenant people, Israel has had an interesting history. But what about the future? What does it hold for this oppressed nation? First of all, the prophetic Scripture declares that *there will always be an Israel.* The giving of the New Covenant was climaxed with these words:

> Thus saith the LORD, which giveth the sun for a light by day, and the ordinances of the moon and of the stars for a light by night, which divideth the sea when the waves thereof roar; The LORD of hosts is his name:
> If those ordinances depart from before me, saith the LORD, then the seed of Israel also shall cease from being a nation before me for ever.
> Thus saith the LORD; If heaven above can be measured, and the foundations of the earth searched out beneath, I will also cast off all the seed of Israel for all that they have done, saith the LORD (Jer. 31:35-37).

Remember that at the time this prophecy was given, the Southern Kingdom of Judah was about to be conquered, destroyed and taken into captivity. The temple and city walls would soon be laid waste. The kingdom would be over, and a period of Gentile dominion (now 2500 years long) was about to begin. This optimistic prophecy was not given at the beginning of a golden era, but at the end. God said that as long as there was a sun, moon and stars there would always be a Jewish nation. He hurled a challenge at mankind to journey to the edge of space or to the center of the earth. As long as this remains a human impossibility, there will always be an Israel. No matter how many Pharaohs, Hamans or Herods there are in the future, they will never be able to annihilate God's Chosen People. The Antichrist will try and fail; so will Satan. But God will preserve His own unto the establishment of that glorious earthly kingdom by His Son.

When the Great Tribulation begins, *Israel will have to be in the land of Palestine.* And she is there now! In 1948 the nation of Israel

was born and guaranteed national integrity by mandate of the
United Nations, with special recognition and protection by the
United States. For the first time since A.D. 70, there was a land that
Jews could call their own. And for the first time since 605 B.C., she
was able to govern her own internal affairs. Israel is now accepted
as a sovereign, autonomous nation by the world club of nations.
The Star of David waves proudly over the Promised Land, and
she has foreign embassies in many of the world's capitals.
Although hated and compressed geographically by her Arab
neighbors, Jews from throughout the free world continue to flood
into the tiny country. A modern exodus has indeed taken place!
God promised: "For I will take you from among the heathen, and
gather you out of all countries, and will bring you into your own
land" (Ezek. 36:24). God has done and is doing just that. It must
be pointed out, however, that Israel is going back to the land in
unbelief. She has not yet acknowledged Jesus of Nazareth as her
Messiah, Savior and King. She has not yet asked forgiveness for
her sin of rejection and crucifixion of God's only Son. She will, but
not until the tribulation period is under way. God said that after
Israel would be brought back into the land *then* He would sprinkle
clean water upon them in order to purify them from their
filthiness (Ezek. 36:25). The important feature of current history
is that there is a nation of Israel in the land of Palestine for the
first time in two millennia.

Although the nation was "re-created" in 1948, it was not until
the summer war of 1967 that she gained *control of and possessed the
old section of the city of Jerusalem.* For almost twenty years, the Jews
had no access to the Wailing Wall and to other revered sites within
the ancient section. They had to be content with the new
Jerusalem as they looked across barriers to their Jordanian
neighbors living where they wanted to be. Imagine the
enthusiasm among Jewry, especially those in Palestine, when
Dayan and his forces marched into the holy city. On their heels
were both liberal and orthodox Jews, crowding their way to the
Wailing Wall and weeping over what had just occurred. In the
years that have followed, the Jews have revamped the city
government, established businesses, and have settled down,
leaving the impression that they are there for good. In fact they
have vowed never to give it up. Both the Pan-Arab alliance and
the United Nations have reacted to this possessive attitude with

pressure upon the Jew to leave. Whether he does is not certain at this time. One thing is sure, however. Jesus said that when the tribulation begins, the Jews will also be in control of the old city:

> And when ye shall see Jerusalem compassed with armies, then know that the desolation thereof is nigh.
> Then let them which are in Judaea flee to the mountains; and let them which are in the midst of it depart out; and let not them that are in the countries enter thereinto.
> For these be the days of vengeance, that all things which are written may be fulfilled (Luke 21:20-22).

This prophecy looked beyond the destruction of Jerusalem by the Romans (A.D. 70) to the end time when Gentile forces would converge upon the Jews and their capital. Could it be that this is the end time and that the geographical stage is set for the tribulation? It is both plausible and possible. Time will tell!

One item is still missing. There is no *Jewish temple in Jerusalem,* and the prophetic Scriptures reveal that there must be one in the great tribulation period. From the call of Abraham to the destruction of Jerusalem (some 2,000 years), the Jews had a place where they could offer animal sacrifices unto God. First, there were the different stone altar sites in the patriarchal age; second, there was the portable Tabernacle from the time of Moses to the construction of Solomon's Temple in Jerusalem; third, Solomon's Temple stood for almost four hundred years before the Babylonians devastated it; fourth, there was Zerubbabel's Temple built after the captivity; and fifth, Herod renovated that Temple, beautified and enlarged it, and it was this Temple that was destroyed by the Romans. For almost 2,000 years now, the Jews have not worshiped God as prescribed in the law.

Some might wonder why a temple was not built after the nation was reborn in 1948. It was because they did not have the old section of Jerusalem in which the site of the two previous temples is located. Now that they have the old city, there has been much speculation over whether Israel will now build the temple. Some have felt that such a temple would unite all Jews everywhere as they have never been united before. However, there are some obstacles. On the temple site now stands a Muslim mosque, a holy place called the Dome of the Rock. This structure would have to be torn down, and one can easily see the immediate Arab rage and the start of another holy war if this happened. Since the United Nations has not recognized Jewish control of this section, it might be folly to start the construction now. Various newspapers and magazines have reported rumors that plans have already been made for the construction of the temple. There was an advertisement in the *Washington Post* which solicited interest and financial help from people wanting to rebuild the temple. Several articles have stated that tons of stone have been ordered from a Bedford, Indiana, quarry. Some have said that the cornerstones are already in Israel.

What does the Bible say about this temple? In the Millennial Kingdom there will be a temple in Jerusalem (Ezek. 40—48). Christ will rule as a King and Priest from that place (Zech. 6:12, 13). However, this temple will be built by the Messiah and inhabited by Him, and it is this temple that must be built upon the original site. It is possible that the Jews could build a temple today on some other site. The Scripture simply states that there will be a temple then; that animal sacrifices will again be offered (Dan. 9:27); that the Antichrist will force the cessation of these sacrifices; that he will enter the temple and set himself up as God and as the object of worship (Matt. 24:15; 2 Thess. 2:4); and that this latter event will take place in the exact middle of the tribulation. Consequently there may be no need for the destruction of the Muslim mosque in order to have the temple. The temple must be built though; this will be the next exciting event in the life of Israel.

Contrary to popular opinion, *Israel will be driven out of the land again.* Jesus said: "And they shall fall by the edge of the sword, and shall be led away captive into all nations: and Jerusalem shall be trodden down of the Gentiles, until the times of the Gentiles be fulfilled" (Luke 21:24). This prophecy went beyond His own day to the tribulation and to the events prior to His second advent to the earth. In the middle of the tribulation, Satan will be cast out of Heaven into the earth. At that time he will energize the Antichrist to break his covenant with the Jews. This false messiah will then set himself up as God in the temple. This will be the signal or sign to the Jews to get out of Jerusalem and the surrounding area (Matt. 24:15-20). John saw that Israel will flee into the wilderness to a place where God will protect her from the wrath of the evil one (Rev. 12:6, 13-17). This will be a time of providential preparation for Israel. During this flight, she will straighten out her theology. She will come to recognize that Jesus is truly her Messiah. She will respond to the declaration of Moses:

> And it shall come to pass, when all these things are come upon thee, the blessing and the curse, which I have set before thee, and thou shalt call them to mind among all the nations, whither the LORD thy God hath driven thee,
> And shalt return unto the LORD thy God, and shalt obey his voice according to all that I command thee this day, thou and thy children, with all thine heart, and with all thy soul (Deut. 30:1, 2).

When Christ comes to the earth after the tribulation, *He will gather the scattered Jews into the land.* The Palestinian Covenant promised that if the Jews repented in their captivity "that then the LORD thy God will turn thy captivity, and have compassion upon thee, and will return and gather thee from all the nations, whither the LORD thy God hath scattered thee" (Deut. 30:3). At this time Israel will look upon their Jehovah-Messiah whom they had pierced at the cross, and they will mourn for Him (Zech. 12:10). This time they will say, "Blessed is he that cometh in the name of the Lord" (Matt. 23:39). When Israel is restored, she will enter fully into the spiritual blessings of the New Covenant:

> A new heart also will I give you, and a new spirit will I put within you: and I will take away the stony heart out of your flesh, and I will give you an heart of flesh.
> And I will put my spirit within you, and cause you to walk in my statutes, and ye shall keep my judgments, and do them.
> And ye shall dwell in the land that I gave to your fathers; and ye shall be my people, and I will be your God (Ezek. 36:26-28).

Now that Israel is spiritually prepared, Jesus Christ will establish the promised kingdom and will personally rule over a redeemed Israel in Palestine.

The future for Israel is both stormy and sunny. Persecution looms ahead, but beyond lies the horizon of the kingdom.

What should be the attitude of Christians toward Israel and

her future? First of all, we should pray for the peace of Jerusalem (Ps. 122:6). We will prosper as we love God's Chosen People and pray for their spiritual welfare. Secondly, we should seek for and pray for their salvation. Paul agonized: "Brethren, my heart's desire and prayer to God for Israel is, that they might be saved" (Rom. 10:1). Within the sovereign purpose of God, there will be national salvation for Israel. But we are still in the Church Age. Every Jew outside of Christ is lost and going to an eternity in the lake of fire. May we try to win some of them to Jesus Christ before it is too late. Thirdly, the present activity in Palestine should cause us to look up to Heaven and watch for His coming. In the Olivet Discourse Jesus issued this parable:

> Now learn a parable of the fig tree; When his branch is yet tender, and putteth forth leaves, ye know that summer is nigh;
> So likewise ye, when ye shall see all things, know that it is near, even at the doors.
> Verily I say unto you, This generation shall not pass, till all these things be fulfilled (Matt. 24:32-34).

This fig tree represents Israel. The putting forth of the leaves could easily represent the establishment of the state of Israel in 1948. If so, then the generation that witnessed this development will be the generation that will be alive at the beginning of the tribulation. The Bible indicates that we cannot know the exact day and hour of His coming, but we can sense the season. How long is a generation? Twenty years? Only that generation twenty years of age and under at Kadesh-Barnea was permitted to enter the Promised Land forty years later. Forty years? During that time, an entire generation perished in the wilderness wanderings. One hundred years? Israel was to be in bondage in Egypt for four generations. It lasted some four hundred years. Are we that generation of which the Bible speaks? It is difficult to say for sure, but it must be admitted that we are living in thrilling, significant times. Child of God, keep your eye upon Israel! It could be later than you think or realize.

8 – WHO IS THE ANTICHRIST?

THE PROPHETIC Scriptures reveal that God has a program which will be climaxed by the coming of His Son, Jesus Christ, into the world to solve the world's ills and to establish a kingdom of righteousness and peace. This same Word tells us that Satan also has a program for the world which will be culminated by the advent of his man, called the Antichrist. Satan is the master counterfeiter. He knows that sinful man needs a person and a program in whom he can put his trust. It is Satan's goal to turn away man's trust from God and to put it in man.

To this end, Satan has designed a false trinity to counterfeit the true Trinity. He takes the place of God the Father; the Antichrist stands in the stead of God the Son; and the false prophet is the opposite of God the Holy Spirit. God's program for the world will be climaxed in the Millennial Kingdom, whereas Satan's program will reach its pinnacle in the Great Tribulation. At that time, the next world dictator will be in power, and men will be so deluded that they will come to accept *the* lie—that a mere man is God. Humanism will reach its peak at the expense of true theism, but that is what people will want and what they will get. How could such a situation develop? Are men that naive and gullible? Jesus said: "I am come in my Father's name, and ye receive me not: if another shall come in his own name, him ye will receive" (John 5:43). Why will this be so? Who could have such worldwide influence? Who is this one who has been dubbed the Antichrist?

At the very start, it must be pointed out that world conditions are very ripe for the entrance of an attractive international leader. Wherever you look, you see war, conspiracy, intrigue, poverty, anarchy and social, political and economic unrest. It was reported that the premier of Belgium, P. H. Spock, made the following statement:

The truth is that the method of international committees has failed. What we need is a person, someone of the highest order or great experience, of great authority, of wide influence, of great energy. Let him come and let him come quickly. Either a civilian or a military man, no matter what his nationality, who will cut all the red tape, shove out of the way all the committees, wake up all the people and galvanize all governments into action. Let him come quickly. This man we need and for whom we wait will take charge of the defense of the West. Once more I say, it is not too late, but it is high time.

Read that quotation over again! The world is desperate, especially the Western world. They want some *one,* and they want him now. Satan knows this; thus the introduction of his man could be very soon. Let us now look at the scriptural description of this coming world leader.

First of all, he will be a Gentile. After predicting the time of the crucifixion, Daniel wrote: ". . . And the people of the prince that shall come shall destroy the city and the sanctuary. . ." (Dan. 9:26). The "people" were the Romans who under Titus devastated Jerusalem and Herod's Temple (A.D. 70). Therefore, the "prince that shall come" must be a *Roman prince.* This means that he will be a European or possibly an American (since the United States is basically an extension of European ideas and peoples). Daniel also saw him as the *little horn* that arose out of the midst of the ten horns which were on the head of the fourth beast (Dan. 7:7, 8, 19-26). This fourth beast represented the iron Roman Empire which followed Greece, Medo-Persia and Babylon in their conquest and control of the Jewish people. In Revelation, the complement of Daniel, John described him as the *beast* rising out of the *sea* (Rev. 13:1-10). In prophetic sections, "sea" represents the vast multitudes of Gentile peoples. Isaiah said of them: "But the wicked [nations] are like the troubled sea, when it cannot rest, whose waters cast up mire and dirt" (Isa. 57:20). The four Gentile oppressors arose out of the sea (Dan. 7). Since the beast of Revelation 13 has the same animal characteristics as they, he also must have a Gentile origin. Many feel that in order to carry off the counterfeit, he must be a Jew, but this is not so. Since he is a fake, he will be a *complete* fake. However, his right-hand man, the false prophet, will be a Jew (Rev. 13:11-18). This prime minister of the false Satanic kingdom will "come up out of the earth," a symbol of the land promised to the Jews.

This coming world leader will doubtless have a dynamic, magnetic personality. He will have that rare ability to move television and radio audiences plus live crowds with his appearance, decorum and eloquent pulpit oratory. He will combine the logic of a Churchill, the emotion of a Hitler and the wit of a Kennedy into a Hollywood-type image. John said that he will have "a mouth speaking great things" (Rev. 13:5). Daniel said that his "look was more stout than his fellows" (Dan. 7:20). He later called him a "king of fierce countenance" (Dan. 8:23). There will be something different about him. Like Saul of old, he will appear to be head and shoulders above all his contemporaries in self-confidence and wisdom. Men will throng to see and hear him. This is not hard to believe in our day of rapid communication and transportation. Wherever world leaders and politicians go, they automatically attract huge crowds. Daniel said that he will be able to understand dark sentences, and that "through his policy also he shall cause craft to prosper in his hand" (Dan. 8:23, 25). It is difficult to say what these dark sentences are, but it is clear that he will have unique wisdom, far superior to others.

The Antichrist will gain world power by two diverse methods—war and peace. In recording his vision, Daniel wrote: "I considered the horns, and, behold, there came up among them another little horn, before whom there were three of the first horns plucked up by the roots" (Dan. 7:8). The divine interpretation stated that he would subdue three kings (Dan. 7:24). In the end time, there will be a ten-nation confederation approximating the land area of the old Roman Empire. The Antichrist will rise to prominence within this alliance by conquering three of the powers, giving him control over the other seven. Now that he has this area of world leadership, he will follow an international policy of peace overtures. In a way, it reminds us of Hitler who ruthlessly gained German power by assassination and then smiled at Chamberlain, saying that he wanted to be at peace with the rest of the world. Daniel said, "And his power shall be mighty, but not by his own power: and he shall destroy wonderfully, and shall prosper, and practise" (Dan. 8:24). He added that "by peace [he] shall destroy many" (Dan. 8:25). The communists also give us an example of those who talk peace at the negotiation table and infiltrate our ranks, carrying a sword at the same time. The word *peace* will be a weapon in his hands. In his rhetorical oratory, he will impress the world that he has the answer for world peace. But as Paul said: "For when they shall say, Peace and safety; then sudden destruction cometh upon them" (1 Thess. 5:3). Peace talk is only a tool to get what he wants. In fact, he will align himself with apostate Christendom in that day to show the world his good intentions (Rev. 17). But once her usefulness is past, he will destroy that church organization. This is why he is pictured as the first horseman of the Apocalypse: "And I saw, and behold a white horse: and he that sat on him had a bow; and a crown was given unto him: and he went forth conquering, and to conquer" (Rev. 6:2). War and peace are the means ("conquering") to the end of world dictatorship ("to conquer").

He will also be intensely anti-Semitic. At first this will not be recognized by the Jews. In fact the Jews will look upon him as the guardian of their national safety. The Antichrist will make a seven-year covenant with Israel (Dan. 9:27) which could be a nonaggression pact. He will guarantee Israel that if any nation comes up against her, he will come to her rescue. There is no indication that the Jews will accept him as their Messiah with the proper prophetic credentials. At the middle of the covenant period, he will break the covenant (diplomatic relations, etc.), invade the land of Palestine, and persecute the Jews. Daniel said: ". . . And in the midst of the week [the seven-year covenant period, the tribulation] he shall cause the sacrifice and the oblation to cease, and for the overspreading of abominations he shall make it desolate" (Dan. 9:27). Jesus referred to this prophecy in the Olivet Discourse and warned the people to flee when they saw the abomination of desolation (the Antichrist) stand in the temple at Jerusalem (Matt. 24:15). John said that he will make war with the Jewish saints and will overcome them (Rev. 13:17; cf. Dan. 7:21). He will also be personally responsible for the martyrdom of the two prophetic witnesses raised up by God in the tribulation period (Rev. 11:7). This will be the greatest Semitic purge of all time, but it will last only three and one-half years (Dan. 7:25).

The basic reason for such oppression of the Jews is the fact that he hates God and His Christ. His great oratory is not only horizontal (aimed at man) but also vertical (aimed at God). "He shall speak great words against the most High" (Dan. 7:25). These great words are really words of blasphemy. John wrote: "And he opened his mouth in blasphemy against God, to blaspheme his name, and his tabernacle, and them that dwell in heaven" (Rev. 13:6). He is a braggart. If anyone ever had a big mouth, he is that person. His verbal darts are hurled not only at God, but at Heaven itself with all of its inhabitants, including the angels and the redeemed Church which had been taken into Heaven at the rapture a few years earlier.

Although his power is mighty, it is not his own power (Dan. 8:24). We are told that "the dragon gave him his power, and his seat [throne], and great authority" (Rev. 13:2). He is definitely energized by Satan. As mentioned in an earlier chapter, after Satan is cast out of Heaven in the middle of the Great Tribulation, he will be so angry at God that he will cause the Antichrist to pour out his wrath upon the Jews (Rev. 12). Paul identified him as the wicked one "whose coming is after the working of Satan with all power and signs and lying wonders" (2 Thess. 2:9). When Jesus claimed to be the Christ, He supported that claim by performing miracles in the power of God through the Holy Spirit. When the Antichrist appears on the scene, he will deceive the world by performing similar miracles, but in the power of Satan. This will be the purpose of Satan—to create such a counterfeit deception that men will accept the lie that the Antichrist is really the Christ. This has always been Satan's method and goal.

> For such are false apostles, deceitful workers, transforming themselves into the apostles of Christ.
> And no marvel; for Satan himself is transformed into an angel of light.
> Therefore it is no great thing if his ministers also be transformed as the ministers of righteousness; whose end shall be according to their works (2 Cor. 11:13-15).

Even the false prophet will do "great wonders, so that he maketh fire come down from heaven on the earth in the sight of men, And deceiveth them that dwell on the earth by the means of those miracles which he had power to do in the sight of the beast" (Rev. 13:13, 14). The forerunner of Christ, John the Baptist, did no miracle, but this one will. In apostolic days, the spirit of Antichrist was seen in the teaching that Jesus was not the Christ, that God the Son had not actually come in the flesh (1 John 2:18, 19, 22; 4:1-3). When the personal Antichrist comes, he will likewise deny that Jesus is the Christ. In addition, could he not also deny the fact that Jesus had come in the flesh a few years before to take away the Church? This would then be a denial of the *physical* second coming which from the time perspective of the Great Tribulation would be a past event.

This miraculous deception will also extend to a counterfeit experience of death and resurrection. John wrote:

> And I saw one of his heads as it were wounded to death; and his deadly wound was healed: and all the world wondered after the beast.
> And they worshipped the dragon which gave power unto the beast: and they worshipped the beast, saying, Who is like unto the beast? who is able to make war with him? (Rev. 13:3, 4).

Rapid communication has enabled the entire world to witness the funerals of great leaders such as John F. Kennedy, Martin Luther King and Robert F. Kennedy. Imagine the awe and wonder if a great world leader, pronounced dead, would suddenly rise from the deathbed or casket! The Antichrist will do exactly this very thing. It is no surprise that the world will wonder at and worship him. They will regard him as indestructible and a man of destiny.

It appears that this death-resurrection episode will occur in the middle of the tribulation since he will immediately become the object of worship and since his power will last for only forty-two more months (Rev. 13:3-5). Paul said that he will oppose and exalt "himself above all that is called God, or that is worshipped; so that he as God sitteth in the temple of God, shewing himself that he is God" (2 Thess. 2:4). The Antichrist will want to be acknowledged as God. He will set up his throne in the tribulation temple, again faking the time when Jesus Christ will rule as God in the millennial temple. All that dwell upon the earth, with the exception of regenerated Jews and Gentiles, will worship him (Rev. 13:8). The false prophet will erect an image, idol or statue to the Antichrist. He will even animate the image, causing it to speak (Rev. 13:14, 15). He will then cause the world to worship the image, and if anyone refuses to do it, he will be killed. Reminds you of the three Hebrew children, the fiery furnace and Nebuchadnezzar's image, doesn't it (Dan. 3)?

Satan will not be left out either, because he will likewise be worshiped (Rev. 13:4). The original sin of Lucifer, who became Satan, was pride. He said: "I will ascend into heaven, I will exalt my throne above the stars of God: I will sit also upon the mount of the congregation, in the sides of the north: I will ascend above the heights of the clouds; I will be like the Most High" (Isa. 14:13, 14). He wanted to receive worship just like God, and in the tribulation, he will realize his selfish ambition. All who refuse to give dual worship to these two personages will either go into the concentration camps, be martyred or flee into the prepared wilderness (Rev. 13:10).

The Antichrist will also be an absolute dictator. In his vision John saw him as a leopard with the feet of a bear and a lion's mouth (Rev. 13:2). These animal characteristics are the same as those found in Daniel's description of Gentile world dominion (Dan. 7). This means that all of the ruthless, bestial traits of past autocratic emperors, kings and dictators can be found in this last world leader.

The Antichrist will control the world of finance and trade:

> And he causeth all, both small and great, rich and poor, free and bond, to receive a mark in their right hand, or in their foreheads:
> And that no man might buy or sell, save he that had the mark, or the name of the beast, or the number of his name (Rev. 13:16, 17).

During the days of Nazi terrorism in Germany, all Jews had to identify themselves by wearing the Star of David. In the tribulation all of his subjects will be marked by the Antichrist. Politically and sociologically, he will seek to change times and laws (Dan. 7:25). The Big Brother of *1984* will actually be here then. He will make the decisions and do the thinking. It will be the duty of the world simply to follow him.

This one will be the total expression of sinful humanity. In his life total depravity will be ultimately realized. Positionally, all men born into the world with an Adamic nature are as bad off as they can be before a holy God; but practically, they are not as bad as they could be. The Antichrist will equate his practice with his position. Take all of the sin of the world; compress it into one human mold; and out will come this wicked one. This is why Paul called him the man of sin and the son of perdition (2 Thess. 2:3).

Because of these titles, some have argued that he will be none other than Judas Iscariot reincarnated. Since Judas was entered by Satan and was called by Jesus "the son of perdition" (John 13:27; 17:12), they must be one and the same. However, there is no scriptural basis for the teaching of human reincarnation. Judgment awaits man after death, not a second visit to the earth (Heb. 9:27). Daniel said that "he shall magnify himself in his heart" (Dan. 8:25). Pride goes before the fall, and this one will have his share of sinful pride.

For centuries Bible students have been intrigued by a certain passage: "Here is wisdom. Let him that hath understanding count the number of the beast: for it is the number of a man; and his number is Six hundred three score and six" (Rev. 13:18). 666! What a number! Man was created on the sixth day, so six is the number of man. But this number is 666, six mentioned three times. What does it mean? The Antichrist will be the ideal man *without God*. He is all that man would be were it not for the providential grace of God. Read this description of the natural man, depraved and guilty before God:

> As it is written, There is none righteous, no, not one:
> There is none that understandeth, there is none that seeketh after God.
> They are all gone out of the way, they are together become unprofitable; there is none that doeth good, no, not one.
> Their throat is an open sepulchre; with their tongues they have used deceit; the poison of asps is under their lips:
> Whose mouth is full of cursing and bitterness:
> Their feet are swift to shed blood:
> Destruction and misery are in their ways:
> And the way of peace have they not known:
> There is no fear of God before their eyes (Rom. 3:10-18).

That passage fits the Antichrist! He is truly the man *of sin* and the son *of perdition*.

If all that the world had to look forward to was the reign of the Antichrist, it would indeed be full of gloom and pessimism. But remember the Biblical axiom: "Whatsoever a man soweth, that shall he also reap." Daniel wrote: ". . . For the overspreading of abominations he shall make it desolate, even until the consummation, and that determined shall be poured upon the desolate" (Dan. 9:27). His judgment will be in kind. He will get exactly what he deserves. His stay upon the mountain peak of human history and glory will be short—only three and one-half years (seven years at the longest). When he dares to defy the second coming of Jesus Christ to the earth after the great tribulation period, he will be finished. Daniel said: ". . . He shall also stand up against the Prince of princes; but he shall be broken without hand" (Dan. 8:25). Paul wrote: "And then shall that Wicked be revealed, whom the Lord shall consume with the spirit of his mouth, and shall destroy with the brightness of his coming" (2 Thess. 2:8).

It won't be much of a contest—a sinful, human monarch against the immortal, incorruptible God-Man, Jesus Christ. At Armageddon (to be discussed later), the career of the Antichrist will end. He will sink into oblivion as other world dictators before him. Both he and his right-hand man will be apprehended and cast alive into the lake of fire burning with brimstone, where they will be tormented day and night forever (Rev. 19:20; 20:10). They will be the first two *human* beings to inhabit this terrible place. The punishment is befitting to the crime. Sin against an infinite, eternal God must require an infinite eternity to carry out the sentence of judgment. The shame is that men and women in that day will willingly follow the Antichrist to the eternal detriment of their souls.

How should the Christian react to this Biblical teaching about the Antichrist? First of all, he should believe it because it comes from God's Word. Secondly, it should quicken his desire *to look up* for "that blessed hope, and the glorious appearing of the great God and our Saviour Jesus Christ" (Titus 2:13). Thirdly, it should burden his heart for the lost of our day lest they enter the Great Tribulation and be deceived by this false messiah. Finally, it should warn us not to speculate about the identity of the Antichrist. In this age of grace, we will not be able to recognize him. He will not be revealed until the tribulation period has started. If someone with spiritual discernment were on earth at the beginning of the tribulation period, he might be able to recognize him. However, the world will not realize his full identity and intention until the middle of the tribulation (2 Thess. 2:2-8). When the Holy Spirit relaxes His restraining force, the Antichrist will be able to pursue his satanic course.

Down through the centuries, men have attempted to equate the Antichrist with a living contemporary. The post-apostolic Christians thought that he was the pagan Roman emperor because they suffered so much at his hands. The Reformation believers claimed that he was the pope of the Roman Catholic Church. In our own century he has been identified with Hitler or Mussolini. Some evangelicals who do not believe in a literal seven-year tribulation period feel that several people could fit the qualifications of the Antichrist, such as one of the Russian premiers or Castro. One Bible educator, back in 1956, identified him as John F. Kennedy. He cited these reasons: his death and "resurrection" as a PT boat commander in the South Pacific during World War II; the requiem mass said for him; and the reception of 666 votes at the 1956 presidential convention.

The famous political prophetess, Jeane Dixon, claimed to have received a divine vision on February 5, 1962.

> A child, born somewhere in the Middle East shortly before 7 A.M. (EST) on February 5, 1962, will revolutionize the world. Before the close of the century he will bring together all mankind in one all-embracing faith. This will be the foundation of a new Christianity, with every sect and creed united through this man who will walk among the people to spread the wisdom of the Almighty Power.

Mrs. Dixon claims that this man's influence will be felt in the early 1980s and that by 1999, the ecumenical religion will be achieved. To the observer from the general public, the prophetic vision might look forward to Utopia, that golden age of unprecedented peace and prosperity. But to the informed Bible student, this prediction points more to a counterfeit religion and kingdom led by the Antichrist.

Child of God, let us not look *around* for the coming of the Antichrist. Let us look *up* for the Savior!

9 – ARMAGEDDON – WHAT IS IT?

THE VERY SOUND of the word *Armageddon* sends shivers up and down the spine of the world. To most political observers and statesmen, it has become a synonym for the end of the world, a universal holocaust, or the total destruction achieved by a thermonuclear war. To these men it would simply be the cold war turned hot, the climactic struggle between East and West, and the end of civilization brought about by men's folly and greed. But, according to them, in the final analysis it would only be a *human* war, caused and fought by human beings only. However, the Scripture defines the battle of Armageddon as a divine-human encounter, with the emphasis upon the divine. Here is how John described the war:

> And I saw three unclean spirits like frogs come out of the mouth of the dragon, and out of the mouth of the beast, and out of the mouth of the false prophet.
> For they are the spirits of devils, working miracles, which go forth unto the kings of the earth and of the whole world, to gather them to the battle of that great day of God Almighty.
> Behold, I come as a thief. Blessed is he that watcheth, and keepeth his garments, lest he walk naked, and they see his shame.
> And he gathered them together into a place called in the Hebrew tongue Armageddon (Rev. 16:13-16).

Armageddon is the "battle of that great day of God Almighty." It is *His* war. He will sovereignly control the wicked ambitions of the future world's leaders by bringing them into the right place at the right time. Only God can turn the wrath of men into His praise (Ps. 76:10). The nations on their own will not destroy the world. That is not God's will. God will conquer the nations at Armageddon, but He will not destroy the world. That will come at a later time (to be discussed in the next chapter).

Great battle names have been enshrined in the war corridors of time—names like Bunker Hill, Valley Forge, Waterloo, Alamo, Little Big Horn, Gettysburg, Chickamauga, Iwo Jima, Battle of the Bulge, Pork Chop Hill and the Vietnamese DMZ. These names, however, will sink into oblivion when Armageddon occurs. There never has been a battle like it and there never will be one after it. It is peculiarly unique. Let us turn now to the Bible for an examination of this titanic conflict.

Where will it take place? Joel located it in the "valley of Jehoshaphat" (3:2). Isaiah extended it to the mountains and even to Edom, which is south of Palestine proper (34:3; 63:1). Zechariah saw that the city of Jerusalem would be strongly involved (12:2). Ezekiel properly summarized the conflict as covering the entire land (38:9). Armageddon literally means "the hill or city of Megiddo." This site was located on the southern rim of the plain of Esdraelon in north central Palestine west of the Jordan River. It was about ten miles south of Nazareth and about fifteen miles from the Mediterranean Sea. Many of Israel's ancient battles had been fought there: Deborah and Barak over the Canaanites (Judg. 4:13); Gideon over the Midianites (Judg. 7); Saul's defeat and death by the Philistines (1 Sam. 31); and the defeat and death of Josiah by the Egyptians (2 Kings 23:29).

Armageddon is the northern gateway to Palestine which is expressly the intersection of three continents: Africa, Europe and Asia. The person or nation that could control the Middle East could certainly rule the world. It is indeed the hub of the earth and the stage on which the final act of the divine-human drama will be played. Because of its strategic position, Palestine has literally become the highway for nations to march into war. The Egyptians, Syrians, Assyrians, Babylonians, Persians, Greeks, Romans, Arabs, Turks and the British have all desired and controlled it at some time. It is no accident that Jesus predicted that "Jerusalem shall be trodden down of the Gentiles, until the times of the Gentiles be fulfilled" (Luke 21:24). This time period is still with us and will be until Armageddon breaks the grip of Gentile world power. John said that the blood of the battle will be visible for 1600 furlongs (Rev. 14:20). This would correspond to the entire length of Palestine, which is approximately two hundred miles from the northern border to the southern. The next great world war, or Armageddon, therefore, will be fought in Palestine, not in Asia, Europe or space.

The next question is extremely vital. When will the battle of Armageddon take place? Some have suggested that it will occur near the end of the Church Age just prior to the rapture. If this be so, then we Christians could have the opportunity (?) of viewing it; however, this destroys the Biblical hope of the imminent coming of Christ for His own. Others have pinpointed it at the beginning of the Great Tribulation, and still others at the end. A few have located it at either the beginning or the conclusion of the Millennial Kingdom. It is difficult to be dogmatic here, but scriptural indications are that it will begin somewhere in the middle of the tribulation period and last until the very end. Armageddon is not a single, isolated battle (like Guadalcanal), but rather an extended campaign (like the South Pacific war theater). It will occur when Israel is dwelling safely in peace in her own land (Ezek. 38:8, 11). This happens in the latter days of Israel's history which Moses identified with the Great Tribulation (Deut. 4:30). The battle will be triggered by the expulsion of Satan from Heaven (Rev. 12:7-13). In his anger he will move the ungodly nations to attack God's Chosen People as they are in the Promised Land. Although we believers will not be on the earth to follow the events of this battle, it is entirely possible that we could see the battle lines forming on the horizon.

In speculating about the participants in a possible World War III, political analysts have matched Russia against the United States, Russia and the United States against Red China, or the white nations against the colored peoples, composed of Black Africans and Orientals. War produces strange bedfellows. In World War II theistic America united with atheistic Russia to fight Germany, Italy and Japan. Those former enemies are now our friends, and Russia has become our cold war foe. So it will be in the end time. Political, economic and racial differences will be set aside when the nations unite to fight against God. Many science fiction stories include the thought that the only thing that could unite a warring human race would be a threat or an invasion from outer space. These writers are very close to the truth. When Jesus Christ descends from Heaven to the earth, leading His army, it will literally be an invasion from outer space. God, in the Person of Jesus Christ, therefore, will be the key participant.

And I saw heaven opened, and behold a white horse; and he that sat upon him was called Faithful and True, and in righteousness he doth judge and make war.

His eyes were as a flame of fire, and on his head were many crowns; and he had a name written, that no man knew, but he himself.

And he was clothed with a vesture dipped in blood: and his name is called The Word of God.

And the armies which were in heaven followed him upon white horses, clothed in fine linen, white and clean.

And out of his mouth goeth a sharp sword, that with it he should smite the nations: and he shall rule them with a rod of iron: and he treadeth the winepress of the fierceness and wrath of Almighty God.

And he hath on his vesture and on his thigh a name written, KING OF KINGS, AND LORD OF LORDS (Rev. 19:11-16).

The second participant will naturally be Israel. Her land area will be the spoil desired by the greedy nations. Christ will come to deliver her from the wrath of these nations. There is no suggestion in the Biblical record that Israel will attempt to defend herself with a military or citizen army. She has done this in her conflicts with her Arab neighbors, but in the Great Tribulation she will be put to hasty flight. Israel, then, will not have an active part in the actual warfare of Armageddon.

Four major national coalitions from the four corners of the globe will press in upon Palestine. The power of the West will be led by the Antichrist (Dan. 9:26). This revived manifestation of the ancient Roman Empire will no doubt include the countries of Western Europe, England and the United States. This would represent the nominal Christian, white segment of the world's civilization. The northern power would be atheistic, communistic, materialistic Russia, plus her satellites (Ezek. 38). Landlocked, she has always desired a highway to the Mediterranean Sea, the Atlantic Ocean and the Indian Ocean, plus the rich oil and mineral treasures of the Near East. The southern force (Dan. 11:5) could represent either the Muslim, Pan-Arab alliance led by Egypt, the nationalistic Black African peoples, or both of them. The Arabs have a death pact to recover Palestine and her holy places from the hated Jews. The Black Africans, if they so desire, can move in only one direction—north. The eastern kingdoms can be seen in the yellow, Oriental peoples of Red China and her neighbors, bound together by race, religion (Buddhist, Confucianist, Shinto) and years of white suppression (Rev. 16:12). As mentioned in an earlier chapter, the stage is prepared; the players are costumed; and the time is near. In the fullness of God's time, the curtain will go up, and the tribulation events, including Armageddon, will take place. In our day the nations seem to be breathing hard with unrest and excitement. Armageddon could be just around the corner.

Now that the location, time and participants have been identified, let us trace the battle movements of the campaign of Armageddon. It must be remembered that the length of the tribulation period is determined by the seven-year covenant made between Israel and the western power led by the Antichrist (Dan. 9:24-27). Because of the perilous international situation, this will probably be a military, nonaggression pact in which the mammoth western power will guarantee the tiny nation of Israel that he will come to her defense if attacked. This will lull Israel into a false sense of security. She may even reduce her military budget in favor of rural and urban economic needs. This may be the human reason why she offers no token military resistence to later attacks.

Both the northern and southern confederations, closest geographically to Palestine, will recognize the easy prey and take advantage of the political situation in Israel. Russia will say: "I will go up to the land of unwalled villages; I will go to them that are at rest, that dwell safely, all of them dwelling without walls, and having neither bars nor gates, To take a spoil, and to take a prey; to turn thine hand upon the desolate places that are now inhabited, and upon the people that are gathered out of the nations, which have gotten cattle and goods, that dwell in the midst of the land" (Ezek. 38:11, 12).

Ezekiel said that the northern army will be massive and mobile and will cover the entire land. Some have suggested that this future war will be fought in ancient ways (foot soldiers using bows and arrows plus horsemen), and that modern, mechanized warfare will be obsolete because of certain antimetallic weapons. However, the prophet could only use the language and vocabulary available to him. He could not mention missiles and tanks when the terms had not yet been coined and would not have been understood by his readers. He was simply directed by the Spirit of God to describe a future battle in the popular terms of his day. Horsemen would imply rapid movement (tanks, planes). Certainly centuries of military techniques will not be discarded when they are desperately needed by these countries.

When the northern power makes its move, it will be joined by the southern force (Dan. 11:40). The situation will look hopeless for Israel because time and geography will appear to be on the side of the north-south confederacy. However, something surprising will happen. God will intervene miraculously. When these armies are upon the mountains of Israel viewing the valley, God will pour out an overflowing rain, hailstones, fire and brimstone upon them. They will be stopped in their tracks, and only a sixth of the army will survive and retreat (Ezek. 38:22; 39:2). This divine judgment will rival that of the destruction of the pursuing Egyptians in the Red Sea (Exod. 14) and the death-sleep of 185,000 Assyrians in one night when the latter had besieged the city of Jerusalem in the reign of Hezekiah (2 Kings 19:35).

God's purpose in destroying the northern power in this unique fashion will be twofold. First, "Thus will I magnify myself, and sanctify myself; and I will be known in the eyes of many nations, and they shall know that I am the LORD" (Ezek. 38:23). Not only will it be a testimony to the nations of the holiness and omnipotence of Jehovah God, but secondly, it will be used to bring about the *spiritual* salvation of the nation of Israel. God said: "So will I make my holy name known in the midst of my people Israel; and I will not let them pollute my holy name any more" (Ezek. 39:7). Also, "so the house of Israel shall know that I am the LORD their God from that day and forward" (Ezek. 39:22). Israel will begin to add two plus two and come up with four. Prophetic Scripture will begin to make sense to her for the first time.

However, Israel will find herself in a paradoxical trap. After being delivered physically from the northern-southern menace and spiritually from her heart blindness, she will find herself the target of the selfish ambition of the Antichrist and of the western confederation. After Palestine is invaded by Russia, the Antichrist will move into the Middle East to protect his interests and to "rescue" Israel as he promised. Subsequently, when the northern army is destroyed from Heaven, he will break his covenant with Israel and seize the land. Daniel wrote:

... And he shall enter into the countries, and shall overflow and pass over.

He shall enter also into the glorious land, and many countries shall be overthrown: but these shall escape out of his hand, even Edom, and Moab, and the chief of the children of Ammon.

He shall stretch forth his hand also upon the countries: and the land of Egypt shall not escape (Dan. 11:40-42).

It may be that the Antichrist will try to take the credit for the annihilation of the northern army. This may be part of the reason why "kindreds, and tongues, and nations" (Rev. 13:7) will submit themselves to his rule and why they will exclaim: "Who is like unto the beast? who is able to make war with him?" (Rev. 13:4). A one-world government will then be set up with the Antichrist as the dictator, ruling out of the temple in Jerusalem. It will be at this time that Israel will flee for her life into the wilderness, possibly into the ancient region of Edom, Moab and Ammon (Dan. 11:41). The political situation will appear extremely secure for the false dictator, but one more ambitious world power remains:

But tidings out of the east and out of the north shall trouble him: therefore he shall go forth with great fury to destroy, and utterly to make away many.

And he shall plant the tabernacles of his palace between the seas in the glorious holy mountain (Dan. 11:44, 45).

What are these "tidings out of the east"? The Antichrist definitely regards them as a threat to his occupancy of the Middle East and therefore sets up his military defenses to repel the attack. The sixth vial judgment (the last before the mention of Armageddon) reads: "And the sixth angel poured out his vial upon the great river Euphrates; and the water thereof was dried up, that the way of the kings of the east might be prepared" (Rev. 16:12). Check a world map, and you will see that the Euphrates River is the natural divider or water barrier between East and West, between the Afro-European world and the Far Eastern Oriental peoples, between the white and the yellow races. Not since Genghis Khan has the East been a threat to the West. But now, in our own time, China has emerged as one of the three great world powers and the one most feared by political friend or foe. In the Great Tribulation, imperialistic China will again be on the move with a massive army provided by her teeming population rate. The stage is thus set for the apparent climactic struggle between two diametrically opposed worlds of race, color and creed.

But it will never take place! Instead they will join forces to fight a common foe, the invader from outer space, even our Lord Jesus Christ. At this time "shall the sun be darkened, and the moon shall not give her light, and the stars shall fall from heaven, and the powers of the heavens shall be shaken: And then shall appear the sign of the Son of man in heaven" (Matt. 24:29, 30). These heavenly phenomena will cause the nations of the world not to fight each other and to ponder their relationship before God. Should they repent and worship God, or should they resist Him? Milton, in *Paradise Lost,* put these words into Satan's mouth: "Better to reign in Hell than to serve in Heaven." These satanically motivated nations will think and do likewise. Natural man is a spiritual rebel. He will do anything but submit his will to that of God. It is a shame, but even God's own children, called Christians, feel and respond in the same way. It is simply caused by selfish human pride, the elevation of the ego. The psalmist recorded this insight into their motivations:

> Why do the heathen rage, and the people imagine a vain thing?
> The kings of the earth set themselves, and the rulers take counsel together, against the LORD, and against his anointed, saying,
> Let us break their bands asunder, and cast away their cords from us (Ps. 2:1-3).

One would think that the nations would repent, especially after a display of divine plagues and judgments; but remember how Pharaoh hardened his heart after the series of ten plagues including the death of his firstborn son? Remember how the Pharisees and Sadducees intensified their conspiracy to crucify Christ even after the latter had raised Lazarus from the dead? Men are no different today and neither will they be then. John wrote that "men were scorched with great heat, and blasphemed the name of God, which hath power over these plagues: and they repented not to give him glory" (Rev. 16:9).

Doesn't it strike you funny that man thinks he can defeat God? A conflict between man and God is like a battle between an ant and an elephant or between a rowboat and a battleship. Can't you just see puny man raising his clenched fist toward Heaven and cursing dares toward God? It would be funny if it were not so tragic *and true!* What will be the response of God? The psalmist added:

> He that sitteth in the heavens shall laugh: the Lord shall have them in derision.
> Then shall he speak unto them in his wrath, and vex them in his sore displeasure (Ps. 2:4, 5).

The sight of finite, mortal men huddled together around Jerusalem in the tiny valley of Jehoshaphat will no doubt be humorous to God Who dwells in all the universe. His humor is balanced, though, by His holiness. He must judge sin and sinners, and He must prepare the earth for the glorious advent of His Son. He has determined that His Son, the true Anointed One, be established as earth's King upon Mount Zion. When Christ asks for His inheritance, the nations will be broken with a rod of iron and dashed in pieces like a potter's vessel (Ps. 2:6-9). The angels will cry to the scavenger birds:

> ... Come and gather yourselves together unto the supper of the great God;
> That ye may eat the flesh of kings, and the flesh of captains, and the flesh of mighty men, and the flesh of horses, and of them that sit on them, and the flesh of all men, both free and bond, both small and great (Rev. 19:17, 18).

There will be no contest. Mortal, corruptible men have no chance against the immortal, incorruptible bodies of the Savior and of His army. There will be no hand-to-hand combat. No shots will be fired. In a moment the battle of Armageddon will be over. All that Jesus Christ has to do is to say the word.

> And I saw the beast, and the kings of the earth, and their armies, gathered together to make war against him that sat on the horse, and against his army.
> And the beast was taken, and with him the false prophet

that wrought miracles before him, with which he deceived
them that had received the mark of the beast, and them that
worshipped his image. These both were cast alive into a lake
of fire burning with brimstone.

And the remnant were slain with the sword of him that
sat upon the horse, which sword proceeded out of his mouth:
and all the fowls were filled with their flesh (Rev. 19:19-21).

The leaders of this human rebellion, the Antichrist and his
prime minister, the false prophet, will be apprehended and cast
alive into the lake of fire, which had been prepared for the Devil
and his angels. John saw them there after one thousand years, and
there they will be forever suffering their just torment (Rev.
20:10). The armies which willingly followed these deceivers will be
put to death by Christ's Word (symbolized by the sword which
came out of His mouth). Their dead bodies will be devoured by
the scavengers, and their souls will depart into Hell. Thus
Armageddon will be over. It will be a day of triumph for heaven
and earth. What a glorious day that will be!

Although Armageddon will be an awesome and terrifying
experience for the world, it should be welcomed by the child of
God as the day of vindication of our holy and sovereign Creator.
Many beneficial results will be produced by this great battle. First
of all, it will mark the end of Gentile world dominion. Jesus said
that Jerusalem had to be trodden down of the Gentiles *until* the
times of the Gentiles had been fulfilled (Luke 21:24).
Armageddon will terminate those times. The colossal image of
Nebuchadnezzar will have indeed been toppled (Dan. 2:1-49).

To this Babylonian king the course of Gentile world rule was
outlined from the conquest of Jerusalem (605 B.C.) to the second
coming of Christ in the form of a metallic image. It was a massive
image, top-heavy and deteriorating from head to foot in quality.
The head of gold represented Babylon, the first power to control
Jerusalem; the silver breast and arms spoke of the Medo-Persian
Empire; the belly and thighs of brass referred to Greece; the legs
of iron were the Roman Empire of Christ's day; and the feet of
iron mixed with clay looked forward to the revived Roman
Empire led by the Antichrist. All of these powers were to have
their share in dominion over God's covenant people in His holy
city. This image would stand until a stone cut out without hands

(Jesus Christ) would smash the image at its feet (referring to the second coming of Christ to the earth at Armageddon). This would cause the image to fall to the ground, to crumble into dust, and to be blown away by the wind, never to be recovered again (signaling the end of Gentile world dominion once and for all).

Nebuchadnezzar saw this period of history as a beautiful statue of military might, but Daniel saw it as a time of ferocious beasts. This holy prophet evaluated the era as God analyzed it—a period when the natural, bestial character of men will manifest itself. The lion, bear, leopard and nondescript beast would correspond to the four metals and countries mentioned earlier. The ten horns rising out of the fourth beast would parallel the ten toes of the feet, stemming from the legs (Dan. 7). Gentile world dominion—sinful, man-centered and anti-supernaturalistic—must come to an end and *will* when Jesus returns to the earth. Then the hallelujah chorus will ring out and bring chills to the spines of the redeemed: "The kingdoms of this world are become the kingdoms of our Lord, and of his Christ; and he shall reign for ever and ever" (Rev. 11:15). The nations will be angry, but we should say with the twenty-four elders: "We give thee thanks, O Lord God Almighty, which art, and wast, and art to come; because thou hast taken to thee thy great power, and hast reigned" (Rev. 11:17).

The judgment of the living nations, or of the sheep and the goats, will also occur at this time. In the Olivet Discourse Jesus spoke of this event:

> When the Son of man shall come in his glory, and all the holy angels with him, then shall he sit upon the throne of his glory:
> And before him shall be gathered all nations: and he shall separate them one from another, as a shepherd divideth his sheep from the goats:
> And he shall set the sheep on his right hand, but the goats on the left (Matt. 25:31-33).

When Jesus returns to the earth, there will still be a great number of people alive, both saved and unsaved. Not all of the unsaved will participate as soldiers in the opposing warring armies; therefore, there will need to be a separate judgment for them. The unsaved soldiers will be put to death on the spot at Armageddon (Rev. 19:21).

In this passage Jesus likened the separation of the living saved from the living unsaved to the division between sheep (saved) and goats (unsaved). To the saved, He will say: "Come, ye blessed of my Father, inherit the kingdom prepared for you from the foundation of the world" (Matt. 25:34). To the unsaved, He will say: "Depart from me, ye cursed, into everlasting fire, prepared for the devil and his angels" (Matt. 25:41). In His parables, Jesus spoke of this event as the separation between the wheat and the tares (Matt. 13:24-30) and the division of good fish from bad fish (Matt. 13:47-52).

The basic issue at this judgment then is: Will a person be permitted to enter the Millennial Kingdom or will he be consigned to the lake of fire? This judgment is not of Jews, but of Gentile *individuals*. Some have thought that this will be a judgment of nations or countries per se and that if a certain country has been friendly to the Jew in the tribulation (like the United States), the entire population of that country, both saved and unsaved, will go into the kingdom. But this is not so. This is an individual judgment, not a national one. The basis of judgment will be faith in Jesus Christ as evidenced by good works of kindness shown toward the persecuted Jews:

> For I was an hungred, and ye gave me meat: I was thirsty, and ye gave me drink: I was a stranger, and ye took me in:
>
> Naked, and ye clothed me: I was sick, and ye visited me: I was in prison, and ye came unto me.
>
> Then shall the righteous answer him, saying, Lord, when saw we thee an hungered, and fed thee? or thirsty, and gave thee drink?
>
> When saw we thee a stranger, and took thee in? or naked, and clothed thee?
>
> Or when saw we thee sick, or in prison, and came unto thee?
>
> And the King shall answer and say unto them, Verily I say unto you, Inasmuch as ye have done it unto one of the least of these my brethren, ye have done it unto me (Matt. 25:35-40).

This oft-quoted passage is also greatly misunderstood. It does not teach salvation by works of charity and kindness. The "least of these my brethren" refers to the Jews of the tribulation who are the kinsmen of Christ according to the flesh. Since the Antichrist will seek to destroy them, they will have to run from place to place seeking refuge and food. Just as in the *Diary of Anne Frank,* there will be Gentiles who will believe in the hope of Israel and who will be opposed to the reign of the Antichrist. These Gentiles will show their faith in the God of Israel by helping the Israel of God. God said to Abraham: "I will bless them that bless thee, and curse him that curseth thee" (Gen. 12:3). True to His promise, God will bring these righteous Gentiles into the Messianic Kingdom. The goats will be those Gentiles who will shut their doors in the face of the oppressed Jews. Their works bear witness to the fact that there never was a time when they accepted the hope of Israel as their personal hope. Thus, at the end of the Great Tribulation, only saved Gentiles will be granted entrance into the kingdom; the unsaved will go into the lake of fire.

The second advent of Jesus Christ will also create the national and spiritual deliverance of Israel. The Jews will have to flee the land when the Antichrist reveals himself, but after Armageddon God will regather them and restore them to the Promised Land. Jesus said that at His coming "he shall send his angels with a great sound of a trumpet, and they shall gather together his elect [Israel] from the four winds, from one end of heaven to the other" (Matt. 24:31). The Old Testament is saturated with passages that refer to this final restoration (Isa. 43:5-7; Jer. 12:15; Ezek. 28:25, 26; Joel 3:1; Zech. 10:10), but Amos really emphasizes its permanence:

> And I will bring again the captivity of my people of Israel, and they shall build the waste cities, and inhabit them; and they shall plant vineyards, and drink the wine thereof; they shall also make gardens, and eat the fruit of them.
> And I will plant them upon their land, and they shall no more be pulled up out of their land which I have given them, saith the LORD thy God (Amos 9:14, 15).

No more pulled out of the land! The Jews have constantly been plucked out of Canaan; they have never enjoyed the land for any great period of time. But then it will be different. Israel is in the land today, but she must go out one more time.

Christ's coming will also produce spiritual deliverance —salvation from heart and mind blindness and from the penalty of sin. Paul wrote: "And so all Israel shall be saved: as it is written, There shall come out of Sion the Deliverer, and shall turn away ungodliness from Jacob: For this is my covenant unto them, when I shall take away their sins" (Rom. 11:26, 27). The New Covenant will indeed be fulfilled at that time (Jer. 31:31-34). At His first advent, the nation cried out: "We have no king but Caesar." However, time and circumstances will change their attitude. At His second coming, they will sing: "Blessed is he that cometh in the name of the Lord" (Matt. 23:39). Rejection will be converted into reception, the cross into a crown, and tears into a smile. A true Israel will finally come to pass. They will not only be the physical seed of Abraham, but they will also be the spiritual child of a believing Abraham. Ezekiel described their experience of regeneration with these words:

> For I will take you from among the heathen, and gather you out of all countries, and will bring you into your own land.
> Then will I sprinkle clean water upon you, and ye shall be clean: from all your filthiness, and from all your idols, will I cleanse you.
> A new heart also will I give you, and a new spirit will I put within you: and I will take away the stony heart out of your flesh, and I will give you an heart of flesh.
> And I will put my spirit within you, and cause you to walk in my statutes, and ye shall keep my judgments, and do them.
> And ye shall dwell in the land that I gave to your fathers; and ye shall be my people, and I will be your God (Ezek. 36:24-28).

No doubt the greatest result of Armageddon and the second advent of Christ will be the establishment of the kingdom of God upon earth. In prophecy this has been called the Messianic Kingdom because Jesus the Messiah will rule over the world. It is called the Millennial Kingdom because in its first phase on this present earth it will be one thousand years long (Rev. 20:1-7). It could also be called a theocratic monarchy because God in the Person of Christ will directly rule over the affairs of men.

The kingdom will be characterized by righteousness, peace and truth. It will be a time when people "beat their swords into plowshares, and their spears into pruninghooks: nation shall not lift up sword against nation, neither shall they learn war any more" (Isa. 2:4). There is a lot of talk about military disarmament and gun control laws, but this will never be achieved this side of the Millennium. In that day there will be no military defense budgets, no West Points, no juvenile delinquency and no violence. It will be an era of peace and prosperity. There will be no welfare rolls or pockets of poverty. There will be material abundance, for the desert will blossom as the rose. The curse upon creation will be partially lifted. Wild animals will again have a domestic nature.

It will be a time when the glory of God will cover the earth even as the waters cover the sea. Christ will be given "dominion, and glory, and a kingdom, that all people, nations, and languages, should serve him: his dominion is an everlasting dominion, which shall not pass away, and his kingdom that which shall not be destroyed" (Dan. 7:14). And we Christians will share in the glory of His reign as His chosen Bride and Queen (Rev. 20:4-6). To live and reign with Him Who loved us and gave Himself for us will be the pinnacle of human experience.

Just a word of caution. Don't be personally guilty of that for which the nations will be accountable at Armageddon. They will be judged for their anti-Semitism, their sinfulness and their rebellion against God. If this is the attitude of your life, then God will have to judge you also. Before that day comes, follow the advice of the psalmist:

> Be wise now therefore, O ye kings: be instructed, ye judges of the earth.
> Serve the LORD with fear, and rejoice with trembling.
> Kiss the Son, lest he be angry, and ye perish from the way, when his wrath is kindled but a little. Blessed are all they that put their trust in him (Ps. 2:10-12).

Yes, kiss the Son! Trust Christ and receive the blessing of imputed righteousness and a right standing before God. Then you will not perish under the wrath of an offended God.

10 – WHEN WILL THE UNIVERSE BE DESTROYED?

IN A NEWSPAPER article entitled "If you would be a prophet, leave little room to hedge," the author cautioned that no person under any circumstances should predict the end of the world and that if he had to do it, he should not set a date. He went on to say that predictions of the end of the world proved to be the Waterloo for many aspiring prognosticators. Several have done just that. They have given their prediction; some have believed them; but the appointed day came and went to the embarrassment of both. In the Dark Ages the world was supposed to come to an end in A.D. 999, so thousands of Europeans sold all that they owned and migrated to Jerusalem. Some thought that the great plague that covered London in A.D. 1665 would destroy the world. It was predicted that the Thames River would overflow its banks, drown London and eventually cover the world on February 1, 1524.

In our own country William Miller said that the world would end on October 22, 1843. Thousands believed him, sold their homes, made special clothing for the eventful day, and then climbed roofs, hills and haystacks to be closer to Heaven on the appointed day. At the end of the day, Miller announced that he had made a faulty calculation and that the *real* end would come one year later. Most of his followers stayed with him, but in another year, he was proved to be a false prophet. More recently the hippie community of California moved to the mountains of Colorado because they believed that the world would end on June 14, 1968. They stated that the asteroid Icarus, a chunk of debris about a half-mile in diameter, would come so close to the earth that it would cause tidal waves and earthquakes, dropping California into the ocean and elevating the lost continent of Atlantis into open view. To them, only Tibet and Colorado would be the safe spots. Icarus did make a pass at the earth, but the closest it came was about four million miles away. Some people were actually worried over the alarms of the hippies, but others just shrugged their shoulders and exclaimed: "We expect that of those kooks."

This is the problem that the Bible Christian faces. How can he warn his friends and relatives to flee the coming wrath and to get ready for the new Heaven and the new earth *without being laughed at?* Perhaps he can't, since "the preaching of the cross is to them that perish foolishness" and since "the natural man receiveth not the things of the Spirit of God: for they are foolishness unto him: neither can he know them, because they are spiritually discerned" (1 Cor. 1:18; 2:14). To the ordinary men on the street, prophets of doom are like the cartoon which they once saw in the Sunday newspaper. It showed a bearded man with long hair, bare feet and sandals, wearing a long white robe, walking up and down Main Street, and carrying a sign which read on one side "The end of the world is near" and on the other side "Eat at Joe's place." Secularism, materialism and a sophisticated, affluent society have produced this kind of atmosphere and a conditioned mind not readily responsive to the divine imperative to repent.

And yet, concerned leaders within the secular world worry about the course of the world. Will humanity destroy itself? According to Arnold Toynbee, twenty-one of the world's civilizations have fallen, nineteen by moral decay and internal corruption and two by conquest. The question is: How and when will this present civilization fall? Nuclear scientists have warned that it is "seven minutes before midnight." They are frightened at the military prospects of a thermonuclear war and they lack confidence in the world's leaders to handle the delicate, potent atom. Jesus said that in the latter days there would be "upon the earth distress of nations, with perplexity" and that men's hearts would fail them "for looking after those things which are coming on the earth" (Luke 21:25, 26). A good serious look at tonight's newspaper or the television news could easily give a sane person a nervous or mental breakdown.

Although he may be laughed at or misunderstood, the involved Christian must speak to the subject of world crisis and the end of the world. He has a "sure word of prophecy," the inscribed Word of God. God has spoken on the subject of the end of the world, and the obedient child of God must relay this information to a world that needs to know. Jesus said: "Heaven and earth shall pass away, but my words shall not pass away" (Matt. 24:35). The Word of God is more enduring than the world of God. But again the question: *When* will this present universe be destroyed?

The Book of Revelation pinpoints the time as after the Millennial Kingdom but during the events of the Great White Throne Judgment. John the apostle was permitted by the Spirit of God to see in rapid succession the great events of the last days. He viewed the second coming of Jesus Christ to the earth after the great tribulation period (Rev. 19:11-16); the battle of Armageddon (19:17-21); the binding of Satan in the bottomless pit (20:1-3); the establishment of the Millennial Kingdom (20:4-6); the satanic led rebellion at the end of the thousand years (20:7-9); and the casting of Satan into the lake of fire (20:10). The next event, the Great White Throne, was introduced in this fashion: "And I saw a great white throne, and him that sat on it, from whose face the earth and the heaven fled away; and there was found no place for them" (20:11).

When God judges the unsaved of all ages, He will also judge this present material world by causing it to go into oblivion, to be renovated and to be molded into the new heaven and the new earth which will be the eternal habitation of God, the holy angels and the saved of all ages. Therefore, the present world cannot be destroyed in our generation by man-caused thermonuclear or germ warfare or by a judgment of God. It cannot blow up before our very eyes. It is at least one thousand years away. No Christian, consequently, can preach that the end of the world *is near.* The world *will* come to an end, but that end is still far away. God plans to accomplish much yet in this battered, sin-sick world.

In the classic Biblical passage dealing with the subject of the end of the world, Peter predicted "that there shall come in the last days scoffers, walking after their own lusts, And saying, Where is the promise of his coming? for since the fathers fell asleep, all things continue as they were from the beginning of the creation" (2 Pet. 3:3, 4). The phrase, "the last days," refers to the last days of the Church Age, and the description certainly sounds like twentieth-century America. People today are self-centered, living for pleasure and for the moment. They are "spending themselves rich" without any thought of a payment day. Modern theology and theologians are bankrupt and apostate. They have denied the

Lord that bought them and have introduced damnable heresies into the church (2 Pet. 2:1). They deny the personal existence of the Biblical God, the Trinity, the incarnation of God the Son, the virgin birth, the essential deity of Christ, His miracles, His subsequent death and His bodily resurrection and ascension into Heaven. It is no wonder then that they deny the physical second advent of Christ ("where is the promise of his coming?") with all of its attendant results.

The Christians of the apostolic era taught that when Jesus Christ returned to the earth, things would be different. The curse upon creation would be partially lifted. The desert would become fertile; wild beasts would automatically become tame; and life spans would be lengthened, comparable to pre-Noahic times. Eventually, however, the universe would be entirely consumed with fire. The unbelievers of that day (and of today too) scoffed at this teaching. It was unthinkable, contrary to the course of history and the laws of nature. They argued that if Christ was going to return to the earth, He would have done it by now (and that was only some thirty years after His death on the cross). Nineteen hundred years have now passed, and their question is still the same: "Why doesn't He come *if* He is coming?" To them, the time lapse is a weakness in the Christian position. They also argue that creation has been undisturbed over the centuries. Today they would be classified as evolutionary and geological uniformitarians. They reject any possibility of a supernatural intervention which could disrupt the normal run of things. According to them, lions have always been wild and carnivorous, and they always will be. Nothing can change their nature. Man has never lived much beyond one hundred years, and he never will. Cemeteries are full of dead people; therefore, there could not be any resurrection of the dead. What they see going on in nature today is what has been and what will be. Christ's return would change that, so they deny that event.

Peter argued that they were wrong on both counts. Creation has been disturbed! But they refuse to admit this. They "willingly are ignorant" of two basic evidences—that of the written Word of God and that of the material world of God (2 Pet. 3:5). Both of these testify to the fact that God judged the human race and disturbed the natural creation in the time of Noah with a universal, cataclysmic flood of water (Gen. 6, 7). Peter wrote, "By the word of God the heavens were of old, and the earth standing out of the water and in the water: Whereby the world that then was, being overflowed with water, perished" (2 Pet. 3:5, 6). The earth is scarred with gorges and canyons caused by swiftly moving currents of water. Rock strata and sedimentations were laid by tidal waves that transported and deposited the components. Fossils, both of plants and animals, speak of a quick burial under great pressure, apart from natural decay and decomposition. The Ice Age with the subsequent change in weather seasons can be attributed to Noah's flood (Gen. 8:22).

Before the deluge, the earth enjoyed a common, subtropical temperature surrounded by a canopy of water which diffused the harmful effects of the sun's rays; therefore, people and things grew larger and lived longer than they do today. But the flood changed all of that! In the nineteenth century, before the introduction of Darwinian evolution, the fossils and the rock strata were believed by unsaved scientists to be the result of a great worldwide catastrophe. Modern geologists, biologists and paleontologists now see them as the result of organic evolution over millions and billions of years. They reject the scriptural interpretation of the fossil record and Noah's time. The Bible says that the water covered all the "high hills, that were under the whole heaven," but the modern scientist and theologian reject this account and call it a myth, legend or fable. They have rejected double evidence, and therefore, they are doubly accountable.

Peter than argued that the same God, Who said that He would destroy the world of Noah and did, has also said that He will destroy the world again, but this time *with fire:* "But the heavens and the earth, which are now, by the same word are kept in store, reserved unto fire against the day of judgment and perdition of ungodly men" (2 Pet. 3:7). In fact, the rainbow is a sign of God's covenant with the earth that He will never again destroy the world with a universal flood (Gen. 9:13-17). The next time that the world is cleansed will be with a bath or a baptism of fire. Peter said that when the end of the world comes, "the heavens shall pass away with a great noise, and the elements shall melt with fervent heat, the earth also and the works that are therein shall be burned up" (2 Pet. 3:10). When the atomic bombs were dropped at Hiroshima and Nagasaki, these verses took on new meaning and significance. For the first time, man held in his hand a tremendous destructive force that came in a small package. When opened, it made a loud sound and generated great heat. It was the tiny atom. But who ultimately controls the atom? Is it not God? He created the universe and the atom and sustains both of them. Christ "uphold[s] all things by the word of his power" (Heb. 1:3). "By him all things consist" or hold together (Col. 1:17). He is the One Who maintains the delicate balance of the electrons, protons and neutrons within the atom. All He has to do is to say the word and the power of the atom would be unleashed everywhere.

Can you imagine what millions and billions of atomic explosions would do to the world? It would be burned up, dissolved. Nothing of the old would be left. The sad feature is that man is "on the beach" of impending divine judgment and is unaware of the approaching clouds of divine fallout. Peter said that the Day of the Lord would overtake the unbelieving world as a thief in the night (2 Pet. 3:10). It will come unexpectedly and as a surprise even though God's Word and His people have warned them about such a day. May more men and women enter into the ark of safety, even Jesus Christ, before the fiery waves of divine judgment cover the earth.

To the Christian, the delay in the Lord's coming or in the final destruction of the world is no problem. Christ will come at the divinely appointed time, and the world will end when God wills it. It is not that it will not happen, or that God is impotent to make it happen, or that God is so sentimental that He cannot bear to punish the world. God simply is not in a hurry, as Peter wrote: "But, beloved, be not ignorant of this one thing, that one day is with the Lord as a thousand years, and a thousand years as one day" (2 Pet. 3:8). God does not reckon time as man does. What is time to an *eternal* God? In Peter's day, thirty years of delay seemed like a long time. It has now been lengthened to almost two thousand years, but what is that to God? To Him, one thousand years ago is like yesterday and two thousand years like the day before yesterday. Thus Christ has only been gone for two days according to the divine calendar. Is that long? Certainly not. Don't rush God.

In fact, the delay is actually a blessing in disguise, but men are too foolish and stubborn to recognize it. Peter added: "The Lord is not slack concerning his promise, as some men count slackness;

but is longsuffering to us-ward, not willing that any should perish, but that all should come to repentance" (2 Pet. 3:9). The delay is an expression of God's grace, mercy, long-suffering, and concern. Every day that the Lord waits in Heaven is another day in which God gives man another opportunity to hear the gospel and to receive Jesus Christ as personal Savior from sin.

When God announced to Noah that He was going to destroy the world, He could have created a great fish to preserve alive Noah and his family (as with Jonah); but He didn't. Why? Because God wanted the wicked people to have a chance to hear the righteous preaching of Noah. In fact, God gave them 120 years in which to repent. Instead, they despised the goodness and mercy of God and mocked Noah. Not one person believed during that lengthy time. God could have judged them without giving them a chance, and He would have remained just and good. He even knew that no one would enter Noah's ark with him, save the family; and yet He gave men more time.

Jonah announced that in forty days Nineveh would be overthrown (Jonah 3:4). God could have judged them without notice, but He didn't. This time the delay started the people to think and to consider their ways. The Assyrians repented, and God spared them.

As you can see, Christ has not come for two millennia because He wants more people to receive Him. When He comes and divine judgment is poured out, then it will be too late. The door to the ark was only open before the rains fell. There was no opportunity to enter after the door was shut by God and after the waters came. God has done everything possible to keep man from going to a Christless eternity in the lake of fire. He loved us so much that He sent His Son to die on the cross for our sins. He has provided a Bible for us in our language so that we can read about His marvelous program of redemption. He has sent preachers to proclaim the good news of the riches of grace in Christ Jesus. He has given us time and opportunities to hear, to think about and to make a weighed decision. He truly is not willing that any should perish. The problem is with man's will, not with God's. Don't criticize God's delay; thank Him for it.

Why is it necessary for God to judge the heavens and the earth? Would it not be sufficient just to punish man for his sin and to allow the righteous then to live in this present universe? Since the universe is inanimate, it never made a moral decision on its own. Why then will it be destroyed by fire? It must be remembered that the first sin was committed in Heaven, in the very presence by God, by Lucifer, the most beautiful and most intelligent of God's angelic creation (Isa. 14:12-15; Ezek. 28:11-19). Satan and the other angels who followed him in his original sin have for millennia lived in the heavens, having access both into the presence of God or the third Heaven and into the earth (Job 1). Heaven has been polluted by their presence. Christ died not only to deliver man from the penalty of Adamic sin, but also to purify Heaven from the pollution of angelic sin (Heb. 9:23). When fallen angels are judged at the day of judgment or the Great White Throne (1 Cor. 6:3; 2 Pet. 2:4; Jude 6), it will be most appropriate that their habitation should also be rid of any aftereffects of their presence.

What about the earth? After the sin and fall of Adam and Eve, God declared to the first man: "Cursed is the ground for thy sake; in sorrow shalt thou eat of it all the days of thy life; Thorns also and thistles shall it bring forth to thee; and thou shalt eat the herb of the field" (Gen. 3:17, 18). The sin of man affected his environment. God did not want a sinful human race to live in a world free of adversity and hard work; therefore, He placed a curse upon the earth, including the plant and animal kingdoms. If sinful man could have lived in an easy atmosphere, he simply would have had more leisure time in which to sin. God knew what was best for man. Actually then, thorns and thistles are a blessing to man's existence on earth as long as he does not have a resurrection body. During the Millennial Kingdom, this curse will be lifted since Christ will be ruling and righteousness will be the order of the day. Paul wrote this passage about that future day:

> For the earnest expectation of the creature waiteth for the manifestation of the sons of God.
> For the creature was made subject to vanity, not willingly, but by reason of him who hath subjected the same in hope,
> Because the creature itself also shall be delivered from the bondage of corruption into the glorious liberty of the children of God.
> For we know that the whole creation groaneth and travaileth in pain together until now (Rom. 8:19-22).

Creation is just waiting for the resurrection of the just. When that occurs, nature itself will be changed and an approximation of the Garden of Eden experience will last for one thousand years. But alas, earth must be purged too because of the polluted presence of both human and angelic sin.

One of the laws of thermodynamics states that although matter cannot be destroyed, the utility of matter decreases with time. The future of the earth and Heaven is therefore bright since God will give them a fresh start. God will mold the old into the new and revitalize it with the presence of Himself and of righteousness. He said: "For, behold, I create new heavens and a new earth: and the former shall not be remembered, nor come into mind" (Isa. 65:17). Revelation 21 and 22 describe the new Heaven, the new earth and the new holy city. They are too extensive to quote here, but read them! They are beautiful! If the old, present universe were able to speak, it would say that it was looking forward to its fiery baptism in order that it might receive the new dress of the eternal state.

What should be the believer's attitude toward the destruction of the world by fire? First of all, he should welcome it and pray for its nearness. Peter wrote: "Looking for and hasting unto the coming of the day of God, wherein the heavens being on fire shall be dissolved, and the elements shall melt with fervent heat? Nevertheless we, according to his promise, look for new heavens and a new earth, wherein dwelleth righteousness" (2 Pet. 3:12, 13). The Christian should desire the day of vindication of our God, a day when every knee shall bow and every tongue shall confess the holy deity of Jesus Christ to the glory of God the Father (Phil. 2:10, 11). Aren't you impatient for the day when you won't hear men take the name of God in vain? Don't you look forward to the time when pornography and dirty novels will be absent from the world? When God judges mankind and the material world, the child of God should be prepared to shout, "Hallelujah, Amen!"

Secondly, if the child of God really believes what God has said, his life will be radically changed. Peter admonished: "Seeing then that all these things shall be dissolved, what manner of persons ought ye to be in all holy conversation and godliness" (2 Pet. 3:11). He added: "Wherefore, beloved, seeing that ye look for such things, be diligent that ye may be found of him in peace, without spot, and blameless" (2 Pet. 3:14). Carnality will disappear, and spirituality will take over. Immaturity will become maturity. Rebellion will yield to complete dedication. Children of a holy God Who will judge an evil world because of His holiness should also be holy in speech and in life.

Our Lord said:

> Lay not up for yourselves treasures upon earth, where moth and rust doth corrupt, and where thieves break through and steal:
> But lay up for yourselves treasures in heaven, where neither moth nor rust doth corrupt, and where thieves do not break through nor steal:
> For where your treasure is, there will your heart be also (Matt. 6:19-21).

The Christian should be Heaven- and God-centered, not earth- and self-centered. He should invest his time, money and effort in indestructible, eternal stocks and bonds which render dividends not only today, but throughout the endless ages. How can a Christian live for earthly, temporal things when those things will be destroyed by fire? Which is more important and has more value? A ranch home with a swimming pool and two cars or establishing mission churches? Being the top insurance salesmen or leading someone to Christ? We are in the world, and naturally we must care about the necessities of life—food, clothing and shelter. But that is not the real issue. Where do your values lie? What are your goals for yourself? For your children? Remember: "Only one life; 'Twill soon be past; Only what's done for Christ will last."

Finally, since God is not willing that any should perish, neither should we. Every day that God delays His judgment is another day for us to be busy about the Father's business. May we pray for and seek to win as many as we can to the Savior before His coming overtakes them.

11 – WHEN WILL BELIEVERS BE JUDGED?

LIFE CONSISTS OF a series of examinations. Throughout elementary, junior-high and senior-high education, the student goes from test to test, anxious and apprehensive about the next report card period. The Olympic figure skater holds her breath at the end of a performance while she waits for the decisions of the judges. The junior executive wonders whether his production and evaluation sheet will be acceptable to his superior. The realm of the spiritual is no exception: "It is appointed unto men once to die, but after this the judgment" (Heb. 9:27).

Although men and women are supposed to judge themselves and be judged or chastised by God in this present world, yet this life must be regarded as probationary and preparatory to the afterlife experience. All judgment is not in this world. There is a judgment to come for both the saved and the unsaved. The judgment in both cases will be severe and serious. Peter wrote: "For the time is come that judgment must begin at the house of God: and if it first begin at us, what shall the end be of them that obey not the gospel of God? And if the righteous scarcely be saved, where shall the ungodly and the sinner appear?" (1 Pet. 4:17, 18). The Christian will be judged, however, before the unsaved stand before God.

The Biblical title for the judgment day of the child of God is "the judgment seat of Christ" (2 Cor. 5:10). In his correspondence with the Corinthian church, Paul emphasized this truth greatly as a cure for church schism and as an incentive to personal witnessing (1 Cor. 3:9-23; 2 Cor. 5:1-11). It is a fact that Christians will be judged after death for their spiritual experience.

When will this judgment take place? In concluding one of His parables, Jesus said: "And thou shalt be blessed; for they cannot recompense thee: for thou shalt be recompensed at the resurrection of the just" (Luke 14:14). Jesus distinguished between two resurrections. The first is the resurrection unto eternal life in which the saved of all ages or those that have done good will participate. The second is the resurrection unto eternal damnation in which the evildoers or the unsaved will be involved (John 5:28, 29). Christ therefore equated the time of the giving of a blessed recompense or reward with the hour of the giving of the resurrected, immortal, incorruptible body. Paul added this thought: "Therefore judge nothing before the time, until the Lord come, who both will bring to light the hidden things of darkness, and will make manifest the counsels of the hearts: and then shall every man have praise of God" (1 Cor. 4:5).

The bodies of the saved will be raised when Christ comes, and that is when the judgment seat will occur. Jesus revealed to John on the island of Patmos: "And, behold, I come quickly; and my reward is with me, to give every man according as his work shall be" (Rev. 22:12). The giving of rewards and the coming of Christ are seen as simultaneous or closely related events. And when is He coming? Could He not come now, this very moment? Is His coming not imminent (see chapter 3)? This is why James admonished his readers: ". . . The coming of the Lord draweth nigh. Grudge not one against another, brethren, lest ye be condemned: behold, the judge standeth before the door" (James 5:8, 9). How would you like to be caught up into the presence of Christ and before His judgment seat while you were arguing with your Christian friends? The Judgment Seat of Christ, therefore, could take place at any moment, even today. It is the next logical event after Christ comes to take the Church into Heaven. It will take place in Heaven during the great tribulation period before Christ comes to the earth after that era. The Church will be evaluated, rewarded and prepared in advance so that she will be able to come with Christ and to reign with Him as His Bride-Queen during the Millennial Kingdom:

> Let us be glad and rejoice, and give honour to him: for the marriage of the Lamb is come, and his wife hath made herself ready.
> And to her was granted that she should be arrayed in fine linen, clean and white: for the fine linen is the righteousness of saints (Rev. 19:7, 8).

In this vision John saw that the true Church, the Bride of Christ, had already made herself suitable for the marriage supper. Her fine linen clothing represented her righteous deeds, performed after salvation, for which she was rewarded. She was ready before Christ's second advent to the earth (Rev. 19:11-16).

Since the event is called the Judgment Seat of Christ, it is obvious that God the Son in His resurrection body will be the Judge before whom all Christians stand. He Himself declared: "For the Father judgeth no man, but hath committed all judgment unto the Son" (John 5:22). This is right. It was the Son Who obeyed the will of the Father and became incarnate through Mary's virgin womb. It was the Son Who was exposed to normal experiences and temptations. It was the Son Who died in the place of sinful men and for sin, Who rose again, Who ascended into Heaven as our divine-human representative and advocate, and Who will return to lead redeemed human beings into the presence of His Father. He understands man fully because He became a man, and today He maintains that humanity. At the end of his life and ministry, Paul challenged Timothy to preach the Word with this incentive: "I charge thee therefore before God, and the Lord Jesus Christ, who shall judge the quick and the dead at his appearing and his kingdom" (2 Tim. 4:1). Yes, one day living (the quick) and resurrected (the dead) Christians will stand *before Christ* to be judged for their service.

How do we know that *only* believers will be judged at the Judgment Seat of Christ? In fact, these are only New Testament believers, those who have received Christ as Savior from the time of Calvary to the rapture of the Church. Old Testament and tribulation saints won't be raised until after the tribulation, so their judgment will of necessity be later. Paul wrote: "For we must all appear before the judgment seat of Christ; that every one may receive the things done in his body, according to that he hath done, whether it be good or bad" (2 Cor. 5:10). Paul said *we;* therefore, he fully expected to be there. In fact, note his repeated usage of the first person plural pronouns (we, our, us) in the following verses:

> For we know that if our earthly house of this tabernacle were dissolved, we have a building of God, an house not made with hands, eternal in the heavens.

> For in this we groan, earnestly desiring to be clothed
> upon with our house which is from heaven:
> If so be that being clothed we shall not be found naked.
> For we that are in this tabernacle do groan, being
> burdened: not for that we would be unclothed, but clothed
> upon, that mortality might be swallowed up of life.
> Now he that hath wrought us for the selfsame thing is
> God, who also hath given unto us the earnest of the Spirit.
> Therefore we are always confident, knowing that, whilst
> we are at home in the body, we are absent from the Lord:
> (For we walk by faith, not by sight:)
> We are confident, I say, and willing rather to be absent
> from the body, and to be present with the Lord.
> Wherefore we labour, that whether present or absent, we
> may be accepted of him (2 Cor. 5:1-9).

These verses describe a Christian, not an unsaved person. No unsaved person has the assurance of a divinely prepared body beyond the grave (5:1). No unbeliever desires life after death to life here on earth (5:2, 3). No unsaved person looks upon death as an entrance into life; to him it is the termination of life (5:4). Only the child of God has enjoyed the inner working of God according to His good will and pleasure (5:5). Only the Christian has the permanent, indwelling presence of the Holy Spirit as a guarantee of future spiritual blessings (5:5). Only the believer is conscious of the fact that he is away "from home," or the presence of the Lord (5:6). The unsaved walk by what they can see and feel; only the Christian walks by faith, taking God at His Word (5:7). Only the child of God lives for the honor and glory of God (5:9). As you can see, *we* can only refer to the redeemed. *All* of the saved of this age will appear there. None will be exempt, from the greatest to the least, from the most spiritual to the most carnal.

Although Christians will stand as one corporate group before Christ, they will not be judged as a group but as individuals. Notice the change from *we* and *all* to *every one*. I will not give an account for you, and you will not give an account for me. I will be judged for my life, and you will be judged for your experience.

In his first Corinthian letter, Paul stated that those who will be judged are they that have been built upon the foundation of Jesus Christ (1 Cor. 3:9-11). This speaks of believers only. The basis of any Christian experience is the Person and work of Jesus

Christ. Upon this cornerstone, the person, the local church and the true Church have been constructed. Thus only genuine possessing and professing Christians of this age will stand at the Judgment Seat of Christ. The unsaved of all ages will appear at the Great White Throne (next chapter).

On what basis will the believer be judged at the Judgment Seat of Christ? Why will he have to stand before God in that day? Will he be there to find out whether or not God will let him enter into Heaven? No, because "he that hath the Son hath life" and he can know absolutely that he has eternal life (1 John 5:12, 13). He is actually there *because* he is saved. Will God punish believers for all those sins which were committed *after* receiving Christ? No, because God has removed all of our transgressions (past, present, future) from us as far as the east is from the west (Ps. 103:12). The believer will never be punished for sins because Christ bore that punishment in His body on the cross. The believer is not under a sentence of penal judgment nor will he enter into judgment because he has found permanent security in Christ and has passed from the sphere of death into life (John 5:24; Rom. 8:1). Some have suggested that the Christian will be punished for all *unconfessed* sin, but Christ paid the penalty for *all* sin, both confessed and unconfessed. Unconfessed sin brings immediate loss of divine blessing to the child of God; this is his loss. For what, then, will he be judged?

Paul wrote: ". . . That every one may receive the things done in his body, according to that he hath done, whether it be good or bad" (2 Cor. 5:10). The believer is going to be judged for the works of his Christian experience done between conversion and death or possibly the coming of Christ. His life before he became a child of God will not be evaluated. He will be judged for what he has done, not for what he has not done. Distinction has often been made between sins of omission and sins of commission, but the emphasis here is on the positive. What have you done for Christ since He has placed life within your soul? What positive contribution have you made to the cause of Jesus Christ and to the honor and glory of God since your release from the shackles of sin?

Paul said that our works will fall into two categories: "good or bad." The word for "bad" here does not mean that which is wicked or sinful. It means something which is worthless or not up to par. In the sport of golf, I have seen a man hit a well-executed shot over a sand trap to within ten feet of the pin. Another man from the same spot will "skull" his ball, causing it to go in a low trajectory. The ball will bounce and bounce, go into the trap, hit against the bank, ricochet toward the hole, and stop within ten feet of the pin. Both men accomplished the same purpose; they put the ball close to the hole. All would agree, however, that one shot was good and the other was poor or bad. So it is in the spiritual realm. The end does not justify the means. God wants to evaluate the "shots" of our lives as well as the end results. We will receive a score for both the number and the types of shots that are made.

Think of Mary and Martha (Luke 10:38-42). Mary was commended by Christ for choosing the *good* part. What did she do? She sat at the feet of Jesus, enjoying His fellowship and eating of the spiritual bread which came out of His mouth. Martha was busy in the kitchen, fixing supper. What Martha did was not sinful or wrong in itself. Most good hostesses would have done the same thing, and this was Martha's protest about her sister. However, there are some things more important, more vital, more life-satisfying than busy work for the Master. To be with Him is better than to serve Him when He wants you at His feet. Mary's action was good; Martha's was bad.

In his first Corinthian epistle Paul contrasted good and bad building materials:

> For we are labourers together with God: ye are God's husbandry, ye are God's building.
> According to the grace of God which is given unto me, as a wise masterbuilder, I have laid the foundation, and another buildeth thereon. But let every man take heed how he buildeth thereupon.
> For other foundation can no man lay than that is laid, which is Jesus Christ.
> Now if any man build upon this foundation gold, silver, precious stones, wood, hay, stubble;
> Every man's work shall be made manifest: for the day shall declare it, because it shall be revealed by fire; and the fire shall try every man's work of what sort it is (1 Cor. 3:9-13).

Paul likened the Christian life to a house built upon the foundation of the Person and redemptive work of Jesus Christ. Each Christian has the responsibility to build upon that foundation a house of character, a life that is well pleasing toward God, a life of value and purpose. The Christian can use good, expensive materials that will pass the test of time and eternity. Paul calls these "gold, silver and precious stones." Or he can use bad, cheap materials like wood, hay and stubble. This passage reminds me of the story of the three pigs and the big bad wolf. Remember how he huffed and puffed and blew down the two houses of sticks and straw, but the house of brick withstood his windy attack? So it is with the life you are building. When God tests it with fire, will it stand or will it go up in smoke? What a tragedy that would be—to live for Christ twenty or forty years and to see it all burn up before your very eyes. All you would have left would be a charred foundation. What a waste!

Notice that God is interested basically in the *quality* of your life, not in the quantity of your works. The fire will try every man's work of *what sort* it is, not *how much* it is. God would rather see a one-room house constructed of gold, silver and precious stones than a thirty-room mansion of wood, hay and stubble. One is valuable because it is built for the honor and glory of God under the direction of the Holy Spirit; the other is simply a monument to self-effort and self-exaltation. Actually, we have little control over the quantity of our works. That is related directly to the number of years that God gives us to serve Him after our conversion. Some are saved late in life and have little time to produce many works. Some are taken home to Glory early in life, either from accident, natural causes or martyrdom. The Ecuador martyrs were cut down by Auca spears in the prime of Christian life and service. They could have produced more works for the Lord, but it was not His will.

God *is* interested in quality, and this is where we have a responsibility. We have something to say about today, about what we are doing with the indwelling Christ-life. Are we yielded to Him? Do we want His will above our will? We can fool men, but we can't fool God. Man looks on the outward appearance, but God looks into the heart. There may be some who are constructing their lives with gold-painted wood and silver-painted stubble. It may look like the real thing, but God is a master jeweler. A simple fire will show up the fake for what it really is. Our work will be "manifested." That means that God will turn us inside out.

Since we Christians one day will have to give an account of our works, it would be well for us to discover what kind of works God will commend and what kind He will criticize. We should know the difference between destructible and indestructible materials, between gold and wood, and between the good and the bad. Let us be master builders for Him. Let our stonecutting, masonry work and carpentry be so excellent that the world will view our good works and glorify our Heavenly Father. The Scripture is saturated with examples of quality spiritual experience. These will serve as general guidelines only.

David wanted to build God a house, but since he was a man of war, that task was reserved for Solomon. After the construction of the Temple, in his sermon of dedication, Solomon reminded the people of David's original request and God's reaction: "And it was in the heart of David my father to build an house for the name of the LORD God of Israel. And the LORD said unto David my father, Whereas it was in thine heart to build an house unto my name, thou didst well that it was in thine heart" (1 Kings 8:17, 18). Did you see the triple mention of "heart"? God was delighted with David's attitude of heart, and although it was not His will, He commended David for his intention. Do you mean to say that God will reward a person for unfulfilled ambition? Yes, that is exactly right. David wanted to build, but he couldn't; he was stopped by the divine purpose.

Within local churches scattered throughout our country, there are men and women who would like to do more for God and His work, but they are unable to do so. Here is a cripple who would love to walk from house to house in order to carry on personal evangelism, but he can't. Here is an elderly gentleman, just saved, who wishes that he could have been converted when he was a young man in order that he might give his life for missionary service, but he can't. Here is a widow who desires to give more money to the work of the ministry, but she can't. God knows this. He will not hold you responsible for what you cannot do; however, He is interested in your heart. If given the opportunity and means, would you give more and go more?

It *is* God's will that every Christian be fully yielded to the indwelling Holy Spirit, ready to do God's will for his life even before it is revealed. It *is not* God's will that every yielded Christian become a full-time missionary, pastor or Christian educator. However, would you be willing to be what He wants you to be, to do what He wants you to do, and to go where He wants you to go? This is the crux of the question. What is the intention of your heart? Remember that "the word of God is quick, and powerful, and sharper than any twoedged sword, piercing even to the dividing asunder of soul and spirit, and of the joints and marrow, and is a discerner of the thoughts and intents of the heart" (Heb. 4:12). God is a spiritual cardiologist; He is interested in the condition of your heart.

Everyone knows the story of the widow and her two mites (Mark 12:41-44). Jesus was interested in how and what the people gave into the temple treasury. He saw that the rich cast in much and that the poor widow put in a couple of pennies. He told His disciples that "this poor widow hath cast more in, than all they which have cast into the treasury: For all they did cast in of their abundance; but she of her want did cast in all that she had, even all her living." How could this be? She did not put in *more* than the others, yet Jesus said that she did. In quantity or amount, she didn't; but in quality, she did. They put in the dividend check, the interest on the savings account, the profit from the sale of a property, and still, they had enough left over to maintain a very high standard of living. The widow put in her bread money, the rent allotment, the clothing allowance. She needed that money to live on, but she wanted God to have it. She was indeed a sacrificial giver; they were not.

In our economy we are impressed with and we honor the philanthropist who donates a million dollars to a new library or hospital. We pass over the five- and ten-dollar checks given by the ordinary man on the street. We are impressed with great amounts; God isn't. Someone once said: "It is not how much of my money I give to the Lord, but how much of His money I keep for myself." Christians squabble over tithing: whether it should be done, whether it should be on the gross or on the net, whether it is for this age, etc. They miss the entire point of giving. Do you give because you *want to,* because you *love* Him? The poor widow did, and she was richer for it.

In the Sermon on the Mount Jesus shocked His listeners when He exclaimed: "Except your righteousness shall exceed the righteousness of the scribes and Pharisees, ye shall in no case enter into the kingdom of heaven" (Matt. 5:20). In Jewish thinking if anybody was going to make it into Heaven, it would be a Pharisee or a scribe. The Sadducees were religious liberals and the Herodians were political opportunists, but the Pharisees were the conservatives or fundamentalists of their day. They believed in God, the existence of angels, the soul, life after death and the inspiration of Scripture. Their lives conformed to the legalistic, Mosaic code. They offered sacrifices, prayed, fasted and gave both to the temple and to the poor. How could Jesus make such a statement? What did He mean? In that same discourse Jesus later explained that their righteousness emphasized the outward veneer, and not the inward essence. In their almsgiving they did it before men, to be seen of men, and to have glory of men. They received men's applause which was their reward; but that was all the reward that they would receive. They would receive none from God (Matt. 6:1-4). When they prayed, they loved to be seen in public places in order to be seen of men. When they fasted, they disfigured their faces to give the obvious appearance of fasting (Matt. 6:5-8). Jesus was not opposed to charity, prayer or fasting. He was not opposed to these virtues being done in public either. He *was* opposed to religious works being done in public just for the sake of being seen. That type will not receive any reward in Heaven. That spiritual exercise was only done for self-exaltation and for self-gratification; it was not performed for the honor and glory of God. True spiritual exercise is done toward God with no thought of human recognition. It is done basically in private, although its influence will be seen in the believer's public deportment. It is this type of work that can be called gold, silver or precious stones. Jesus said that this secret work would be rewarded openly by the Father Who knows all things.

Paul said that a child of God should not sit in judgment upon his brother's actions and attitudes in the area of Christian liberty: "But why dost thou judge thy brother? or why dost thou set at nought thy brother? for we shall all stand before the judgment seat of Christ" (Rom. 14:10). Christian liberty deals with the area of nonmoral issues or mores and of questionable amusements. There are no situation ethics in the realm of absolute morals decreed by God, but in unrevealed, not forbidden questions there can be a difference of opinion between two believers. It is in this area that there is a lot of misunderstanding and misrepresentation. Paul warned us that we should not be judges and reminded us that one day we will give an account *of ourselves* to God (Rom. 14:12). Do you attend the movie theater? Selected movies? Do you dance? Modern? Square? Do you play cards? Whether you answer in the positive or in the negative, you must be prepared to tell Christ why you did or didn't participate. Did He give you the freedom to do so? Did you exercise your freedom wisely and without offense to your Christian brother and without loss of testimony to your unsaved friend? Did you do it for God's ultimate honor and glory? God will want to know your inner motivation and the desired goal of the exercise of your freedom in questionable areas.

What will be the results of the Judgment Seat of Christ? What effect will it have on the believer? Paul wrote:

> If any man's work abide which he hath built thereupon, he shall receive a reward.
> If any man's work shall be burned, he shall suffer loss: but he himself shall be saved; yet so as by fire (1 Cor. 3:14, 15).

The Christian will receive or suffer the loss of a reward at that day. He will *not* receive or suffer the loss of salvation then. This is impossible. Even if his entire work for Jesus Christ should be burned (notice that it is his *work* which is burned not the man himself), he will still be saved (1 Cor. 3:15). Why? Because the pure foundation of Jesus Christ is still standing. This cannot be taken away. He will get into Heaven by the skin of his teeth, but he will be there. He will be ashamed of the fact that he has nothing of value to present to the Savior, but he is still God's child, and God will permit him to enter that eternal home. Any spiritual effort done in the energy of the flesh will be consumed; only Holy Spirit prompted work will be rewarded.

The giving of rewards really manifests the nature of the judgment seat (*Bema* in the Greek). This was the term used of the place where the Olympic judges stood to reward the contestants who had excelled in their athletic games. If the athlete ran according to the rules and won, then he was granted an award, usually an olive wreath or crown that was placed upon the head.

Paul used this metaphor in taking inventory of his ministry:

> Know ye not that they which run in a race run all, but one receiveth the prize? So run, that ye may obtain.
>
> And every man that striveth for the mastery is temperate in all things. Now they do it to obtain a corruptible crown; but we an incorruptible.
>
> I therefore so run, not as uncertainly; so fight I, not as one that beateth the air (1 Cor. 9:24-26).

The Greek athletes worked for temporal awards; the Christian should work for eternal rewards.

The Bible identifies these rewards as crowns. In the above passage, Paul mentioned the *incorruptible crown*. This is given to the Christian who practices self-control or discipline in his spiritual life and service. It is given to the believer who excels in spiritual dedication. It is given to the triumphant one, not to the also-ran or mediocre believer. Carnal, immature, backslidden church members have no chance for this award. It is given to the one who has endured hardness as a good soldier of Jesus Christ, who has not entangled himself with the affairs of this life, and who has striven for mastery (2 Tim. 2:3-5). This motto was displayed in my high school gymnasium: "A winner never quits, and a quitter never wins." To win, you must persevere and finish. The Christian race is not a one-hundred-yard dash; it is the twenty-six-mile marathon. Only proper diet, exercise, sleep and practice can produce a winner for that event. Few Christians, doubtless, will qualify for this crown.

The *crown of rejoicing* will be given to the Christian who has been faithful in soul winning and witnessing for Christ. Paul regarded the Thessalonian converts who had been saved through his ministry (Acts 17) as his crown: "For what is our hope, or joy, or crown of rejoicing? Are not even ye in the presence of our Lord Jesus Christ at his coming? For ye are our glory and joy" (1 Thess. 2:19, 20). A living organism should reproduce, and like should produce like. A Christian in whom the living Christ dwells should seek to win others to the Savior. When the hymn writer entitled his song "Nothing but Leaves," he referred to the episode when Christ sought fruit from a tree but found only leaves. Will we have fruit to place into the nail-scarred hands of Christ, or will there be only leaves? What a joy it would be at the Judgment Seat of Christ to point to some for whom we had prayed, to whom we had witnessed, and who received Christ as a direct result of our interest!

Paul looked forward to his martyrdom because he knew that he had done his work well and that death would take him into the presence of Christ whom he dearly loved. And yet he still anticipated Christ's return: "Henceforth there is laid up for me a crown of righteousness, which the Lord, the righteous judge, shall give me at that day: and not to me only, but unto all them also that love his appearing" (2 Tim. 4:8). This *crown of righteousness,* therefore, will be given to the Christian who remains morally and doctrinally sound and who is looking for and loving the appearing of Christ. Love for Him will produce love for His return; and love of His coming will keep one in the faith.

The *crown of life* will be awarded the Christian who endures temptations and trials out of love for Christ (James 1:12). This person rejoices when God tests his faith because through this experience he will be able to learn more of God's sustaining grace. It will be an opportunity to enter into the fellowship of His sufferings. Many believers have been subjected to ridicule and physical harassment and have borne it well. They rejoiced because God counted them worthy to suffer shame for His name (Acts 5:41).

To the faithful pastor Christ, the chief Shepherd of the sheep, will give a *crown of glory* that will not fade away (1 Pet. 5:4). The qualifications are these:

> Feed the flock of God which is among you, taking the oversight thereof, not by constraint, but willingly; not for filthy lucre, but of a ready mind;
> Neither as being lords over God's heritage, but being ensamples to the flock (1 Pet. 5:2, 3).

He must provide spiritual food for mature Christians and for young converts (John 21). He must guide the sheep into green doctrinal and moral pastures. He must enjoy his work. He must be a director, not a dictator. This award, apparently, is only for those who are in the full-time ministry.

What should be the attitude of the Christian toward the

Judgment Seat of Christ? First of all, it should motivate him to get busy for the Lord. Paul wrote: "Knowing therefore the terror of the Lord, we persuade men" (2 Cor. 5:11). Paul wanted to be a better ambassador for Jesus Christ because he knew he would have to give an account to his superior in his home country one day (2 Cor. 5:20). Secondly, he should desire the greatest commendation that Christ could give to an individual: "Well done, thou good and faithful servant." It is a paradox, but if we do anything that is good or faithful, it is because God has worked in our lives and made it possible. And yet God will thank us for doing it. Third, it should come as an encouragement to the child of God that Christ will find something in all of us to commend. Paul said that in that day every man shall have praise of God (1 Cor. 4:5). It is a good psychological and educational principle to commend before you criticize. Christ did this in the seven letters to the seven churches of Asia (Rev. 2, 3). If a person has been truly regenerated, then there has been a time when he has produced genuine works of righteousness (James 2). For these, at least, he will be commended. Finally, the Christian should not desire the crowns selfishly. He should look upon them as something that he can cast before the heavenly throne in open submission and thanksgiving (Rev. 4:10). Christ is the One Who is worthy to receive glory, honor and power. May God grant that we have much to give Him in that blessed day.

12 – WHAT ABOUT THE GREAT
WHITE THRONE JUDGMENT?

FOR YEARS the common view about the future was basically very simple. After Jesus Christ returned to the earth, He would judge all men, both the saved and the lost, at one general judgment. The unsaved would be cast into Hell, and the children of God would go into Heaven. Thus the new Heaven and the new earth would be instituted. However, God's prophetic program is more sophisticated than that. Whenever the Bible speaks of a judgment to come, it doesn't always refer to the same judgment, as we have seen in the earlier chapters. When Christ became sin and took the place of sinners on the cross, God judged sin in His Son at Calvary (2 Cor. 5:21). He suffered the infinite, eternal wrath of God in a few hours for all of us.

The believer has the privilege and responsibility of self-judgment (1 Cor. 11:31). To have a sensitive spiritual experience, he must examine his heart and mind to see whether there is any unconfessed, unforsaken sin there. If he finds some, he should confess it, and God will both forgive and cleanse him (1 John 1:9). If the believer knowingly and persistently sins before God without repentance, then God will judge him in this present life with chastisement (1 Cor. 11:32; Heb. 12:3-11). It is done for the Christian's welfare; but it is only of personal value if the erring child learns from the experience.

In the last chapter we saw that all believers of this Church Age will stand at the Judgment Seat of Christ to be evaluated for their works (2 Cor. 5:10). During the Great Tribulation, God will judge His covenant nation and will purge out the rebels among Israel (Ezek 20:33-38). At the end of the tribulation when Jesus Christ comes to the earth, He will judge all living Gentiles, permitting some to enter the Millennial Kingdom and casting others into Hell (Matt. 25:31-46).

But the one judgment that captures the imagination and

interest of both the sacred and secular worlds is that great climactic judgment called the Great White Throne. Here is John's full description of that event:

> And I saw a great white throne, and him that sat on it, from whose face the earth and the heaven fled away; and there was found no place for them.
>
> And I saw the dead, small and great, stand before God; and the books were opened: and another book was opened, which is the book of life: and the dead were judged out of those things which were written in the books, according to their works.
>
> And the sea gave up the dead which were in it; and death and hell delivered up the dead which were in them: and they were judged every man according to their works.
>
> And death and hell were cast into the lake of fire. This is the second death.
>
> And whosoever was not found written in the book of life was cast into the lake of fire (Rev. 20:11-15).

The first obvious question to ask of that event is: When will it take place? John saw the judgment as occurring *after* the one-thousand-year rule of Christ on the earth but *before* the introduction of the new Heaven and the new earth (Rev. 21:1). The time scheme of the Book of Revelation is both logical and chronological. The Church was outlined in the seven letters to the seven churches (Rev. 2:1—3:22). The Great Tribulation with its seal, trumpet and vial judgments is described in chapters 4—18. John then saw in a vision the second coming of Christ to the earth (19:11-16); the battle of Armageddon (19:17-21); the binding of Satan in the bottomless pit (20:1-3); the Millennial Kingdom (20:4-6); the release of Satan and the subsequent rebellion of mankind (20:7-9); and the casting of Satan into the lake of fire (20:10). It is at this juncture that John describes the Great White Throne. The eternal state is depicted afterwards (21:1—22:7).

Where will the judgment take place? John said that at the time it was occurring, the earth and the heaven were fleeing away (Rev. 20:11). In chapter 10 (of this book) this "fleeing" referred to the destruction of our universe by fire. The only adequate answer, then, is to say that it will be staged in space. It will not happen in our present universe, either on earth or in the atmospheric, stellar or divine heavens. No planet in our solar system will qualify. It could take place somewhere beyond our universe that has not been affected by angelic sin. Whether the assigned place actually exists today, it is hard to say.

Who will be the judge? John ambiguously stated that he saw the Great White Throne and *him* that sat on it (20:11). In the next verse, he identified *him* as God. But which Person within the triune Godhead? The Father? The Son? Or the Holy Spirit? In His earthly ministry, Christ stated that the Father had committed all judgment into His care (John 5:22). Although it is difficult to distinguish among the ministries of the three Persons, special emphasis is given to one more than the other. For instance, all three Persons had a share in the resurrection of Christ. The Father raised Him (Acts 2:24), the Son raised Himself (John 10:18), and the Spirit raised Him (Rom. 1:4; 8:11); but the emphasis seems to be upon the Father.

When Paul was invited to preach to the Athenian philosophers on Mars Hill, he commanded them to repent "because he [God] hath appointed a day, in the which he will judge the world in righteousness by that man whom he hath ordained; whereof he hath given assurance unto all men, in that he hath raised him from the dead" (Acts 17:31). Jesus Christ is *that man.* He became man, died for men, rose in a resurrected, immortal, incorruptible, glorified human body, ascended into Heaven, and serves as our mediator and intercessor before God. Christ did not throw off His humanity at the cross or in the tomb. He is forever joined to it.

According to Jesus, the Holy Spirit today is laying the groundwork for the future judgment by the Son:

> And when he [the Holy Spirit] is come, he will reprove the world of sin, and of righteousness, and of judgment;
> Of sin, because they believe not on me;
> Of righteousness, because I go to my Father, and ye see me no more;
> Of judgment, because the prince of this world is judged (John 16:8-11).

All three categories (sin, righteousness and judgment) relate to the Person and passion of Christ. If an unbelieving world will not submit to the Spirit's witness to Jesus Christ today, then it will have to confront the Savior face to face at the Great White Throne. He is the executor of divine justice. He indeed will tread the winepress of the fierceness and wrath of Almighty God (Rev. 19:15).

John said that he saw the *dead* stand before God (Rev. 20:12). Who are these dead? They are participants in the second resurrection. It is a Biblical fact that all human beings who have died will be raised from the dead, but they will not all be resurrected at the same time. Daniel wrote that "many of them that sleep in the dust of the earth shall awake, some to everlasting life, and some to shame and everlasting contempt" (Dan. 12:2). Jesus complemented this prophetic passage with these words:

> Marvel not at this: for the hour is coming, in which all that are in the graves shall hear his voice,
> And shall come forth; they that have done good, unto the resurrection of life; and they that have done evil, unto the resurrection of damnation (John 5:28, 29).

There are two resurrection groups. The first are those saved ones who have done good and who will share God's life with Him. The second refers to the evildoers or the unsaved who are destined to shame, everlasting contempt and damnation.

How do we know that they will not all be raised at the same time? Christ, nineteen hundred years ago, was the firstfruits of the first resurrection (1 Cor. 15:20). His victory guarantees our triumph over the grave. Paul said that "in Christ shall all be made alive. But every man in his own order: Christ the firstfruits; afterward they that are Christ's at his coming. Then cometh the end, when he shall have delivered up the kingdom to God, even the Father" (1 Cor. 15:22-24). God is orderly. Just as Israel marched, tribe by tribe, family by family, through the wilderness, so God has an order of resurrection. The true Church, composed of all believers from the Day of Pentecost to the rapture, will be raised and caught up to meet the Lord at the beginning of the tribulation period (1 Thess. 4:13-18).

All Old Testament saints will be resurrected at the conclusion of the tribulation (Isa. 26:19; Dan. 12:1-3). So will the tribulation martyrs be raised then. John saw "them that were beheaded for the witness of Jesus, and for the word of God, and which had not worshipped the beast, neither his image, neither had received his mark upon their foreheads, or in their hands" (Rev. 20:4) ready at the beginning of the Millennium to reign with Christ. John wrote: "Blessed and holy is he that hath part in the first resurrection: on such the second death hath no power, but they shall be priests of God and of Christ, and shall reign with him a thousand years" (Rev. 20:6). The first resurrection involves all of the above-mentioned groups: Christ, the Church, pre-Calvary saints, and the tribulation saved dead. Because they have been justified by faith, they indeed are blessed, holy and free from eternal damnation.

John then observed that "the rest of the dead lived not again until the thousand years were finished " (Rev. 20:5). The "rest of the dead" in this verse is the same as "the dead" who stand at the Great White Throne. Here John clearly describes a time difference between the two resurrections. The first will be completed by the beginning of the Millennial Kingdom, whereas the second will occur after Christ's earthly reign. Since the second death, or eternal separation from God in the lake of fire, will befall the participants in the second resurrection (Rev. 20:6), the dead at the Great White Throne must be the unsaved. All of the unrighteous of all ages from Cain to the millennial rebels will be there. Both the small and the great of this life (as men view other men) will be there: the banker and the beggar, the prince and the pauper, the statesman, the scientist, the lawyer, the doctor, the professor, the author, the mechanic, the housewife, the bricklayer, the farmer and the criminal. In this life men have station, but before Christ there will be no respect of persons. Although they will stand there en masse, they will be judged individually (note the change from "the dead" to "every man," Rev. 20:13).

These dead will have come from either a watery ("the sea") or an earthly ("death") grave. God will raise their bodies and unite them to their souls which have been in Hell ever since their physical death (Rev. 20:13). When an unsaved person dies today, his body is placed into the casket, but his personality or conscious self goes to Hell or Hades (the English transliteration of the Greek word which means "the unseen place"). There, unseen to the earthly human eye, he is aware of his desperate plight (Luke

16:19-31). He is in torment in his intermediate body, the body which the soul has between death and resurrection. He is conscious of the presence of others. He remembers his earthly experiences and has concern for the spiritual welfare of his lost relatives and friends. He is unable to change his position before God. When Christ speaks, all of the unsaved dead will respond. None can stay in Hades. All will stand in a new, resurrected body before the Lord at the throne.

The Scriptures also indicate that the fallen angels, including the demons and evil spirits, will be judged at this time. Their leader, Satan, has already been consigned to the lake of fire (Rev. 20:10). He had already been judged and sentenced at Calvary's cross; this event simply carried out the sentence of judgment. The angels which corrupted the world of Noah and which had been chained in darkness ever since will be there (2 Pet. 2:4; Jude 6). Apparently we Christians will have a share in judging the fallen angels, probably because they have been a source of temptation to us (1 Cor. 6:3).

The threefold power of Satan, the grave and Hell will not be able to prevent the unsaved from being resurrected when Christ gives the word. He has the keys of Hell and death by virtue of His death and resurrection (Rev. 1:18). When Christ died on the cross, His body was placed into the tomb and His soul went into Hell (Acts 2:27-31). He went into the bowels of darkness from which no man before Him had ever returned. He went into Satan's realm, the power of death. It is not that Satan had the power to slay anyone, but he had the power to keep human beings in the realm of death. There could be no uniting of a new body with the human spirit until someone had conquered him. This Jesus did. He went into Satan's house, snatched the keys of Hell and death out of his hand, and walked out in triumph over sin and death. Whenever Christ wants to use those keys, He can, and Satan will not be able to do anything about it. Christ became man "that through death he might destroy him that had the power of death, that is, the devil; And deliver them who through fear of death were all their lifetime subject to bondage" (Heb. 2:14, 15). In His passion He indeed spoiled spiritual principalities and powers and publicly ridiculed and exposed them by triumphing over them in it (Col. 2:15). No unsaved person will be able to resist the call to be resurrected and stand at the Great White Throne.

The unsaved will be judged on the basis of the contents of certain books—the Book of Life (singular) and the books of works (plural). John wrote: ". . . And the books were opened: and another book was opened, which is the book of life: and the dead were judged out of those things which were written in the books, according to their works" (Rev. 20:12). What is the purpose of the Book of Life? It contains the names of all who have fully trusted God for their salvation. After the disciples returned from a successful preaching and healing mission, Jesus said to them: "Notwithstanding in this rejoice not, that the spirits are subject unto you; but rather rejoice, because your names are written in heaven" (Luke 10:20). Possession of salvation is a greater joy than the promotion of service. Paul was convinced that the names of his fellow laborers were in the Book of Life (Phil. 4:3). John said that only those "whose names are not written in the book of life of the Lamb slain from the foundation of the world" (Rev. 13:8) would worship the Antichrist. God will show to the unsaved person that there never was a time when he genuinely received His Son, Jesus Christ, as his personal Savior. At the Great White Throne, some will profess to have salvation who actually do not possess eternal life. The condition of their hearts is different than the confession of their lips. Jesus mentioned such people in His Sermon on the Mount.

> Not every one that saith unto me, Lord, Lord, shall enter into the kingdom of heaven; but he that doeth the will of my Father which is in heaven.
> Many will say to me in that day, Lord, Lord, have we not prophesied in thy name? and in thy name have cast out devils? and in thy name done many wonderful works?
> And then will I profess unto them, I never knew you: depart from me, ye that work iniquity (Matt. 7:21-23).

It is possible to name the name of the Lord and to carry on a ministry in His name, and yet miss Heaven and salvation. Jesus did not deny the fact that they had done these things in His name; He denied that He ever knew them. There was no personal, intimate relationship. They were strangers to His grace. Their hypocrisy was indeed gross iniquity. Judas was a perfect example of this type of person. He traveled with the Lord for over three years; he preached, healed and taught under the authority of Christ; and yet, he was never saved. In speaking to His disciples in the upper room, Jesus remarked: "Ye are clean, but not all. For he knew who should betray him; therefore said he, Ye are not all clean" (John 13:10, 11). Judas was indeed the son of perdition, bound for the lake of fire. It cannot be argued that Judas once knew the Lord but later lost his salvation. Speaking of the lost, Jesus said that He *never* knew them. If they had been saved at one time, He could not have used the word *never*.

Peter spoke of those who became entangled again with the pollutions of the world which they had once escaped through the knowledge of Christ (2 Pet. 2:20). They had entered into the fringe benefits of Christianity but had never enjoyed the true inner essence. Their natures had never been changed. They were like the dog who ate his vomit and like the hog which went back into the mudhole. Their outward cleansing and inner relief from pollution were only temporary.

In this way John described apostates: "They went out from us, but they were not of us: for if they had been of us, they would no doubt have continued with us: but they went out, that they might be made manifest that they were not all of us" (1 John 2:19). Lack of continuance within the moral and doctrinal framework of the true Church was an indication that the person had never really identified himself with God or His people.

A person therefore will be cast into the lake of fire because his name is not mentioned in the Book of Life. But what is the reason for the other books? These books record the works of the person's earthly experience. They reveal his unrighteous deeds and thoughts, his rejected opportunities to receive the gospel, and his degree of sinfulness in relation to the other unsaved people. Just as the believer at the Judgment Seat of Christ receives degrees of rewards on the basis of his works, so the unbeliever at the Great White Throne will receive degrees of punishment in the lake of fire on the basis of his sinful works.

Do you mean to say that there are degrees of sins and that there will be degrees of punishment? Yes, that is exactly right! But isn't all sin the same? Isn't all punishment the same? No, this is a popular misconception. Sin is sin, but still there are varying degrees. When Jesus stood before Pilate on the day of His crucifixion, He declared: ". . . He that delivered me unto thee hath the greater sin" (John 19:11). The sin of the Jewish leaders was greater than the sin of the Roman governor. It is true that Pilate should not have condemned an innocent man to death, but he did it out of political expediency to appease the demanding crowd. The Pharisees and the Sadducees should have known better. They knew the Old Testament Scriptures. The Messianic prophecies were indeed fulfilled in Jesus of Nazareth, and yet they rejected the evidence of His sinless Person, His gracious words and His works of healing. They were more blameworthy because to whom much is given, much is expected. God had revealed to them more truth than to the pagan Gentiles. They rejected this truth and *the* Truth, Christ (John 14:6); therefore, their sin was greater and their punishment more severe.

During His earthly ministry, Jesus criticized the cities for their rejection of Him:

> Then began he to upbraid the cities wherein most of his mighty works were done, because they repented not:
>
> Woe unto thee, Chorazin! woe unto thee, Bethsaida! for if the mighty works, which were done in you, had been done in Tyre and Sidon, they would have repented long ago in sackcloth and ashes.
>
> But I say unto you, It shall be more tolerable for Tyre and Sidon at the day of judgment, than for you.
>
> And thou, Capernaum, which art exalted unto heaven, shalt be brought down to hell: for if the mighty works, which have been done in thee, had been done in Sodom, it would have remained until this day.
>
> But I say unto you, That it shall be more tolerable for the land of Sodom, in the day of judgment, than for thee (Matt. 11:20-24).

Did you catch that phrase, "more tolerable in the day of judgment"? The ancient cities rejected the messages of godly prophets and angelic messengers to repent, but these first-century cities rejected the very message of God Himself in the Person of Jesus Christ. The latter were given more light, but they loved darkness more than light. For this reason their punishment will be more severe in the outer darkness of eternity.

The principle that degrees of punishment are based upon the

severity of the crime was put forth by Christ in His parable of the steward and his two servants. Here is the conclusion:

> And that servant, which knew his lord's will, and prepared not himself, neither did according to his will, shall be beaten with many stripes.
> But he that knew not, and did commit things worthy of stripes, shall be beaten with few stripes. For unto whomsoever much is given, of him shall be much required: and to whom men have committed much, of him they will ask the more (Luke 12:47, 48).

Christ contrasted "few" stripes with "many" stripes. The degrees were based upon relative knowledge and ignorance of the master's will. Throughout history there have been those who had a greater knowledge of God's will and His program of salvation. The American has had every opportunity to hear and to believe. Evangelical churches are everywhere; Bibles can be purchased in any bookstore; the gospel can be heard on most radio and television stations, especially on Sunday. He has no excuse for rejecting Christ. His punishment in the lake of fire will be more severe than the ignorant bushman who lives in the heart of Africa, South America or Australia. This latter person may live from the cradle to the grave and never see a Bible in his own language or hear the gospel from the lips of a missionary. Nevertheless, he is still a guilty, lost sinner because he has rejected the revelation of God contained in nature and within his very being (Rom. 1, 2).

After every unsaved person has received his sentence of punishment, all the unbelievers will be cast into the lake of fire. John observed: "And death and hell were cast into the lake of fire. This is the second death" (Rev. 20:14). The lake of fire is a real place, not a state of mind. God prepared it for the Devil and his angels (Matt. 25:41), but man can choose to go there by rejecting Christ.

Some have questioned the literalness of the fire. Is it real fire, or is it simply symbolic language? Assuming that it is metaphor, remember that God selects His symbols intelligently. The torment that men will experience will be more like that which comes from *heat* than from *cold*. The eternity for the lost is more like an incinerator than a blinding snowstorm. Actually, there is no good reason to deny the literalness of the lake of fire. If real, resurrected human bodies will go into a real Heaven, then a real Satan, real fallen angels and real bodies of the lost will go into a real place, called the lake of fire.

How can a human body live in a sea of fire without being consumed in a few minutes? The natural bodies which we now inhabit could not survive, but remember that the unsaved are going to receive new bodies. They will not be glorified bodies, fashioned to the image of Jesus Christ, but they will be of such a composition that they will be able to endure forever the fiery torments without being destroyed. God preserved the three Hebrew children in the midst of Nebuchadnezzar's furnace (Dan. 3). The intermediate body of the rich man did not perish in the torment of Hell (Luke 16). So it will be in the lake of fire. God will match the fire with the resurrected body of the unsaved.

Some have wrongly stated that the unsaved will spend eternity in Hell. Hell or Hades is not the eternal abode of the lost; the lake of fire is. The unsaved go to Hell at death to wait for the second resurrection and the Great White Throne. John said that both death and Hell would be cast into the lake of fire (Rev. 20:14).

It is at this time that men will experience the second death. When Adam sinned in the Garden of Eden, he died spiritually and began to die physically. All future generations were born in Adam's likeness, in a state of spiritual death with a body destined to die. All men apart from Christ are dead in trespasses and sins (Eph. 2:1). They are without God, or separated from Him, in this life. When a person dies, his soul separates from his body. Separation is the essence of death. The second death, therefore, refers to the eternal separation of the person, both body and soul, from the presence of the living God.

In the lake of fire man will live with the conscious agony that he is forever estranged from God and that he cannot do anything about it. No wonder there will be weeping and gnashing of teeth. These people will not be angry at God, nor will they curse His name. They will be angry at themselves for rejecting God's gracious offer of salvation in favor of selfish pursuits.

There is no indication in the scriptural record that men will protest, argue or complain about God's decision at the Great White Throne. The rich man in Hell did not feel that his torment was undeserving. Paul said that in the future "every knee should bow, of things in heaven, and things in earth, and things under the earth; And that every tongue should confess that Jesus Christ is Lord, to the glory of God the Father" (Phil. 2:10, 11). Even unsaved men will have a new perspective after their resurrection. They will recognize the sovereignty of God. They will acknowledge that God has been just in His dealings with them and that their fate is deserving. But it will be too late to change their eternal destiny.

What kind of people will occupy the lake of fire? Notice John's description: "But the fearful, and unbelieving, and the abominable, and murderers, and whoremongers, and sorcerers, and idolaters, and all liars, shall have their part in the lake which burneth with fire and brimstone: which is the second death" (Rev. 21:8). In that listing the unbelievers are numbered right along with the morally wicked. You don't have to be a great sinner to get into the lake of fire; you just have to an unbelieving sinner.

Friend, if you have never received Jesus Christ as your personal Savior, won't you do it now? "He that believeth on him is not condemned: but he that believeth not is condemned already, because he hath not believed in the name of the only begotten Son of God" (John 3:18). If you receive Him into your life, you will never come into condemnation because you will have passed from the sphere of spiritual death into the sphere of everlasting life (John 5:24). The person who is in Christ Jesus will never have to stand before God at the Great White Throne (Rom. 8:1). Do it! Receive Him before it is too late!

13 – WHAT SHOULD THIS BOOK
DO FOR YOU?

NOW THAT YOU have come this far, ask yourself these questions: What have I read? What has it done for me? The world cynically defines a prophet as a man who knows tomorrow why the thing he predicted yesterday did not come true today. It believes that a prophet never can tell for sure why his prediction came true or why he failed. It would regard this type of a book as a religious novelty. Is that your feeling? If so, you are badly mistaken. The author does not claim to be a prophet or the son of a prophet. These are not his ideas basically. He has simply tried to be an exegete of Scripture. He has tried not to read into the Biblical record any preconceived notion of the future. He has endeavored to lead out the true scriptural meaning and intention. He has tried to correlate all relevant texts on certain themes into one organic whole. He has made an effort to let the Bible speak for itself on these important issues.

The Biblical prophets did not experience any failures in their foretelling. They met with success every time. History has confirmed the accuracy of their writings. With them, there was no "may" or maybe." Every oracular statement was introduced by "thus saith the Lord." They did not originate these prophecies; they were divinely given by God Who knows the end from the beginning.

One key purpose of this volume, therefore, was to inform the reader about God's prophetic program for the future. Men have listened to other men too much and too long; they need to listen to Him Who has governed the past and Who controls the future destiny of the world. Looking ahead, the child of God can see on the horizon between time and eternity the imminent coming of Jesus Christ to catch the true Church into Heaven; the Great Tribulation with its divine judgments and the manifestation of the Antichrist; the clash between the nations and Christ's army at

Armageddon; the establishment of the Millennial Kingdom of righteousness and peace; the last human rebellion led by Satan; the Great White Throne; the fiery purge of the old heavens and earth; and the entrance of the eternal state with its new heavenly and earthly conditions. However, it is hoped that this study has not merely been an academic adventure. May it have gone beyond the head to the heart.

The second major purpose, and no doubt the most important, was to lead the reader into a greater and more vital experience with God through our Savior, Jesus Christ. History—past, present and future—is His story. Unless one sees Him and sees Him clearer, the study has been in vain. It is the author's hope, first of all, that if you have not had a life-transforming experience of regeneration through acceptance of Jesus Christ as Savior from personal sin, you will believe on Him Who is interested in your spiritual welfare both today and tomorrow. Do it now; don't delay! Secondly, the author trusts that the child of God will have been brought into a more mature relationship with Christ. May you have greater faith in the promises of God. May a new holiness have been instilled into your being. May you have a greater love for Christ, for your brethren in the Lord and for a lost and dying world. May you be filled with comfort and optimism in knowing that the future rests within the hands of God. May your work for God increase within your local church. May you have a greater desire to honor and glorify God in all that you do and think.

In closing, may all of our hearts and minds be saturated with the prospects of seeing our blessed Redeemer, Jesus Christ, face to face:

O blessed hope! O blissful promise!
Filling our hearts with rapture divine;
O day of days! hail Thy appearing!
Thy transcendent glory forever shall shine!
He is coming again, He is coming again,
The very same Jesus rejected of men;
He is coming again, He is coming again,
With pow'r and great glory, He is coming again!

Even so come, Lord Jesus! Amen!

QUESTIONS FOR DISCUSSION

Chapter 1

1. How can prophetic truth be used effectively in personal evangelism? In public evangelistic meetings?

2. Do current evangelical films which use a prophetic theme go beyond the clear teaching of Scripture? If so, what can be done to correct the erroneous impressions left with the viewer?

3. When should Christian young people be introduced to the doctrine of eschatology? As primaries? Juniors? Early teens? Are there any dangers in talking about the doctrines of death and Hell to the very young?

4. Should evangelicals consult the horoscope? Display the signs of the zodiac?

5. What should be the proper Biblical attitude toward such phenomena as ESP, parapsychology and other forms of clairvoyance?

Chapter 2

1. Are Christians ignorant of scriptural support for the second coming of Christ? From the Old Testament? From the New? What can be done to correct the situation?

2. If a person denies the reality of Christ's second advent, can he really be saved?

3. Is it more difficult to believe in the reality of Christ's second coming today than it was in the first century? Why? Can this difference be seen in the behavior of modern believers?

4. How should the Christian view reports of the appearances of Christ to individuals? Seen on earth? In the clouds? In dreams?

5. Is there too much preaching on the Second Advent today? Too little? How can balance be achieved?

Chapter 3

1. Is it right for churches and groups of churches to limit membership in their bodies to those who hold the same beliefs about the doctrine of last things?
2. To what extent should church members be exposed in differing eschatological beliefs? In books? In invited speakers?
3. Do Christians really believe that Christ could come today? What has detracted from belief in imminency?
4. Do many Christians look upon the imminent coming of Christ as an event which will interrupt their own plans? For marriage? For vocation? For retirement?
5. In what ways has faith in Christ's imminent return kept you from sin? Be specific in your personal illustrations.

Chapter 4

1. What is the universal Church? The local church? What is the relationship between the two?
2. Are modern funerals Christian? How can they be improved?
3. Do Christians face death with proper Biblical perspective? How can children be taught about the reality of death?
4. Do people understand the proper relationship of the spirit to the body? Do they overemphasize the body? The spirit?
5. Are modern believers looking for the blessed hope? What has taken away their love for this event?

Chapter 5

1. What characteristics of tribulations in this life are similar to those of the Great Tribulation? Which are different?

2. If the posttribulational position were correct, how would it affect the outlook and behavior of believers today?

3. Is evangelism more effective in times of persecution? Defend your answer.

4. Why do some believe that the world will get better and better? Is there any basis for the world to have optimism about its future?

5. Do you think that people who have rejected the gospel message in this age will be able to accept Christ during the tribulation? How does one's answer to this question affect his evangelistic approach today?

Chapter 6

1. In what ways are messages about the signs of the times misunderstood and abused by both preachers and laymen? What can be done to correct the situation?

2. How should current events be interpreted by the serious student of Bible prophecy?

3. How should the establishment of Israel as a nation and the emergence of the superpowers be viewed? Are they the fulfillment of specific prophecies?

4. How should a study of the signs of the times affect the behavior of Christians? Is it beneficial? Harmful?

5. Why have popular presentations of prophetic events (e.g., the works of Hal Lindsey) been so appealing, both to Christians and the unsaved alike?

Chapter 7

1. Should Christians go on tours to Israel? What would be the benefits? Any drawbacks?

2. Should Christians support the actions of the modern state of Israel regardless of what she does? What about raids into other countries?

3. Does Israel have to rebuild the temple in Jerusalem before the rapture of the Church can take place?

4. Should Christians ask their congressmen to support all arms programs to Israel? Should they be against all military support for Arab nations?

5. How can a premillennial Christian use his prophetic convictions in his witness to unsaved Jews? Are premillennialists more effective in Jewish evangelism than amillennialists?

Chapter 8

1. What characteristics of the Antichrist can be seen in certain world leaders today? In the lives of the unsaved?

2. What conditions prevalent in the world today are conducive to the rise of a man like the Antichrist?

3. What part will apostate Christendom play in the emergence of the Antichrist? How can believers remain in antichristian denominations?

4. Should believers try to identify the Antichrist? Is harm done to the evangelical cause by equating him with Hitler, Kennedy, Kissinger or others?

5. How can the miracles performed by God's power be distinguished from those done by Satanic energy? In what ways can believers be deceived?

Chapter 9

1. What is the proper Biblical attitude toward war in general? The wars of Old Testament Israel? Modern Israel?

2. Can a Christian serve in the armed forces in all capacities? Can he justify pacifism?

3. Has the alignment of world powers today ever been seen in the history of the planet? Does this mean that the world is very near to Armageddon?

4. Is it true that those who are ignorant of history are bound to repeat it? What should Christians learn from ancient and modern history?

5. In what ways should preachers criticize the actions of the United States and the United Nations?

Chapter 10

1. How active should a Christian be in the ecological control of his environment? Should he protest the pollution of the air and the waters?

2. In what ways do Christians lay up treasures on earth? Are most believers more earthly minded than heavenly minded?

3. Is the world really afraid of a thermonuclear war that will destroy the human race and the productivity of the planet?

4. How can the Christian use the destruction of the world as an evangelistic tool? As a means of edification?

5. Can a genuine Bible Christian hold to an evolutionary explanation for the origin and the termination of the universe?

Chapter 11

1. Why do some believe that they can eventually lose their salvation?

2. What are some modern, specific illustrations of works that would be classified as gold and silver? As wood and stubble?

3. Why do Christians continue to judge each other according to outward appearance? What things which are paised by man are actually condemned by God?

4. Do Christians fear the Judgment Seat of Christ like Paul did? What has caused the difference?

5. Are evangelists and soul winners (those who harvest) magnified beyond others? How can the importance of each ministry be equalized?

Chapter 12

1. Are the unsaved of today aware of their sinfulness? How do they define or explain their wrongdoing?

2. Do people today believe in life after death? In future judgment? In punishment such as the lake of fire?

3. How can eternal punishment be reconciled with the truth that God is a loving God?

4. What determines the differences in sin? If sin is sin, how can one sin be greater or worse than another?

5. Is the lake of fire a literal place? Is the fire real or symbolic? How could anybody exist in such a place?